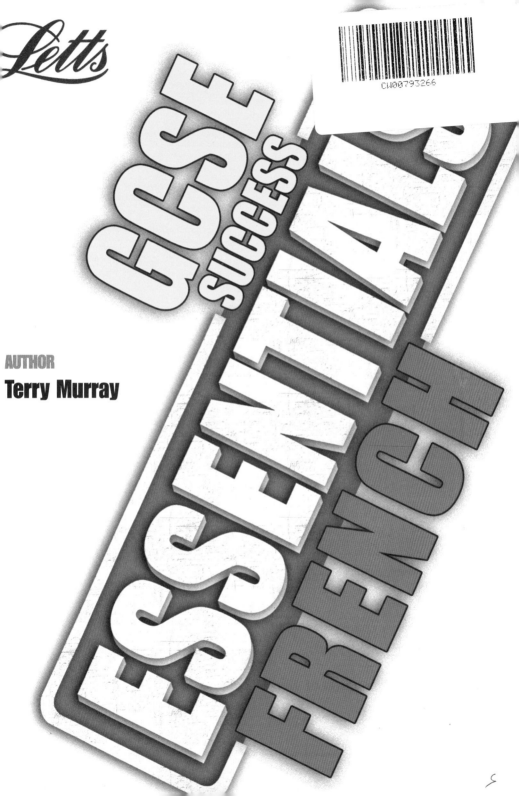

Letts

GCSE SUCCESS ESSENTIALS FRENCH

AUTHOR

Terry Murray

Introduction

Contents

Vocabulary

Grammar

Coursework

Contents

Introduction

About this book

This book complements the **GCSE French Success Guide** and the **GCSE French Success Questions and Answers**. It has been written by a Chief Examiner and it includes useful examiner's tips, with emphasis on areas that students find difficult.

Quick reference

Keep the book to hand during French lessons, while doing your homework and when revising for your GCSE French exams. It contains all the vocabulary and grammar that you need to know, model role-plays and advice on coursework.

Tackling the tricky areas

Each year, your exam board writes a report on how candidates coped with the GCSE exam that year. It identifies areas in which students did badly and areas in which they did well. This report is sent to your school. The areas of difficulty are usually the same year after year, and many of those are addressed either in this book or in the range of other Letts GCSE French titles.

KEY

(f) = feminine noun
(m) = masculine noun
Feminine adjective endings are given in brackets. e.g. cassé(e), beau (belle)

Keys to success

In your GCSE exam, you have to do a listening test, a reading test, a speaking test and either a writing test or writing coursework. Each of the four tests counts for 25% of the total marks. Here are a few tips to help you revise for these tests.

Vocabulary

You cannot expect to do well in any of your GCSE tests if you have not learned the vocabulary. Each exam board issues a list of vocabulary to schools. Their exams are based on this list of vocabulary: if a word is in the list, it can be tested, and if it is not in the list, it cannot be tested. **The words in this book are drawn from the exam boards' lists, so you can be sure that a lot of them will be tested in your GCSE exam.**

Learn as much vocabulary as you can. Find out by trial and error how many words you can learn in a 15-minute session. Most people can learn 10 words.

1 Look at the word, cover it with your hand and see if you can say it from memory. Lift your hand and see if you got it right. This process is called RaCaSaC (Read, Cover, Say, Check).

2 Look at the word, cover it with your hand and see if you can write it from memory. Lift your hand and see if you got it right. This process is called RaCaWaC (Read, Cover, Write, Check).

3 When you think you know the 10 or so words, go away and do something else. Then come back a few minutes later, cover the French – **not the English!** – and see if you can write out all 10 French words.

Grammar

You cannot get the highest grades in your GCSE exam unless you are familiar with French grammar. Work through the grammar section in this book point by point. Tackle approximately one grammar point in a 15-minute session and re-read it until you understand it. When you come to the verb sections, make sure you learn the irregular verbs. (For learning tips, see **Vocabulary** above.)

Coursework

Read through the coursework section in this book before doing your first piece of coursework. It gives you some essential advice and points out what makes a piece of coursework good. It also presents a sample piece of coursework. Why not build up your own collection of coursework fragments? You could call it your 'coursework survival kit'. Every time you come across an impressive word, phrase or structure, write it down in your survival kit. When writing your coursework, use as many items from your survival kit as you can.

Role-play

In your speaking test, you will have to do either one role-play (AQA exam board) or two (all the other boards). Practise the role-plays in this book. It is more fun if you can do this with a friend. Keep repeating the candidate's words until you can look at the English prompts and say all the French responses without looking at the suggested answers.

Good luck!

Days, months, seasons

Days

les jours de la semaine (m)	the days of the week
lundi	Monday
mardi	Tuesday
mercredi	Wednesday
jeudi	Thursday
vendredi	Friday
samedi	Saturday
dimanche	Sunday

Seasons

les saisons (f)	the seasons
le printemps	spring
l'été (m)	summer
l'automne (m)	autumn
l'hiver (m)	winter
au printemps	in spring
en été/ automne/hiver	in summer/ autumn/winter

Months

les mois de l'année (m)	the months of the year
janvier	January
février	February
mars	March
avril	April
mai	May
juin	June
juillet	July
août	August
septembre	September
octobre	October
novembre	November
décembre	December

JUIN

Useful expressions

bonjour!	good morning!
bonne journée!	have a good day!
en juillet/ au mois de juillet	in July
lundi	on Monday
le lundi	on Mondays/ every Monday
tous les jours	every day
toute la journée	all day

Numbers

zéro	0	quatre-vingt-dix	90
un/une	1	cent	100
deux	2	cent un	101
trois	3	cent quatre-vingt-dix	190
quatre	4	deux cents	200
cinq	5	deux cent onze	211
six	6	mille	1 000
sept	7	deux mille	2 000
huit	8	un million	1 000 000
neuf	9	la dizaine	about ten
dix	10	la douzaine	dozen
onze	11	premier/première	first
douze	12	deuxième	second
treize	13	troisième	third
quatorze	14	quatrième	fourth
quinze	15	cinquième	fifth
seize	16	sixième	sixth
dix-sept	17	septième	seventh
dix-huit	18	huitième	eighth
dix-neuf	19	neuvième	ninth
vingt	20	dixième	tenth
vingt et un	21	onzième	eleventh
vingt-deux etc.	22	douzième	twelfth
trente	30	dix-septième	seventeenth
quarante	40	dix-huitième	eighteenth
cinquante	50	dix-neuvième	nineteenth
soixante	60	vingtième	twentieth
soixante-dix	70	vingt et unième	twenty-first
soixante et onze	71	cinquantième	fiftieth
quatre-vingts	80	centième	hundredth

Time, negatives

Time

l'heure (f)	the time
Quelle heure est-il?	What's the time?
Il est sept heures	It's seven o'clock
Il est deux heures cinq	It's five past two
Il est neuf heures et quart	It's a quarter past nine
Il est quatre heures et demie	It's half past four
Il est six heures moins vingt	It's twenty to six
Il est une heure moins le quart	It's a quarter to one
Il est midi/minuit	It's twelve noon/midnight
Il est midi et demi	It's half past twelve (noon)
Il est minuit et demi	It's half past twelve (midnight)
à seize heures vingt-cinq	at 16.25
du matin	a.m.
de l'après-midi	p.m. (until 5 p.m.)
du soir	p.m. (after 5.p.m.)
à cinq heures du matin	at five o'clock in the morning
Quelle est la date d'aujourd'hui?	What's the date today?
C'est le lundi treize janvier deux mille cinq	It's Monday the thirteenth of January 2005
mille neuf cent quatre-vingt-seize/ dix-neuf cent quatre-vingt-seize	1996
le dimanche premier mai	Sunday the first of May

Negatives

ne … aucun(e)	no	ne … plus	no more/no longer
ne … jamais	never	ne … que	only
ne … ni … ni …	neither … nor …	ne … rien	nothing
ne … pas	not	ne … non plus	neither
ne … personne	nobody	pas de (vin)	no (wine)

Quantities, 'Avoir' expressions, question words

Quantities

autant (de ...)	as much	la moitié (de ...)	half (of ...)
une boîte de ...	a box of ...	un morceau de ...	a piece of ...
une bouteille de ...	a bottle of ...	un paquet de ...	a packet of ...
le centimètre	centimetre	la plupart (de ...)	most (of ...)
un demi-/ une demie-	half a ...	un pot de ...	a pot of ...
une douzaine de ...	a dozen ...	un quart (de ...)	a quarter (of ...)
entier (entière)	whole	un tiers (de ...)	a third (of ...)
une goutte de ...	a drop of ...	une tranche de ...	a slice of ...
pas grand-chose	not much	un peu (de ...)	a little
une livre de ...	a pound of ...	un peu plus	a little more
		une paire de ...	a pair of ...

'Avoir' expressions

avoir besoin de ...	to need
avoir envie de ...	to want (to do something)
avoir faim	to be hungry
avoir l'air (malade)	to look (ill)
avoir lieu	to take place
avoir mal à ...	to have a pain in ...
avoir peur	to be frightened
avoir raison	to be right
avoir soif	to be thirsty
avoir sommeil	to feel sleepy
avoir tort	to be wrong
en avoir marre	to be fed up

Question words

à quelle heure?	at what time?
à qui?	whose?
avec qui?	with whom?
combien de fois?	how often?
combien de temps?	how long?
combien?	how much?/ how many?
comment?	how?
où?	where?
pourquoi?	why?
qu'est-ce que?	what?
qu'est-ce qui?	what?
quand?	when?
qui est-ce qui?	who?
qui?	who?
quoi?	what?

Everyday life
Home life

Home life

At home

l'air *(m)*	appearance	intérieur(e)	*internal/inside*
l'ampoule *(f)*	light bulb	à l'intérieur	*indoors*
l'appartement *(m)*	flat/apartment	la lampe	*lamp*
le balcon	balcony	la lumière	*light*
la boîte aux lettres	letter box	la machine à coudre	*sewing machine*
la cave	cellar	la maison	*house*
le chauffage (central)	(central) heating	les meubles *(m)*	*furniture*
chez moi	at home, to/at my house	meublé(e)	*furnished*
		la moquette	*carpet (fitted)*
l'entrée principale *(f)*	main entrance	le pas	*step*
l'escalier *(m)*	stairs	la pendule	*clock*
extérieur(e)	external/outside	les pièces *(f)*	*rooms*
à l'extérieur	out of doors	le placard	*cupboard*
la fenêtre	window	le plafond	*ceiling*
le fond	bottom/far end	le plancher	*floor*
le garage	garage	la porte	*door*
le gaz	gas	la poubelle	*dustbin*
la grille	gate (metal)	le premier étage	*first floor*
l'habitude *(f)*	habit	le rez-de-chaussée	*ground floor*
l'horloge *(m)*	clock	le rideau	*curtain*
		le salon	*sitting room*
		le sommeil	*sleep*
		le tapis	*carpet (not fitted)*
		le toit	*roof*
		le vestibule	*hall*
		le volet	*shutter*

Tip These words are often tested in the listening and reading tests.

VOCABULARY

10

For more help see **Success Guide** page **9**

The living room

la salle de séjour	the living room
le canapé	settee
le CD	CD
la chaîne hi-fi	hi-fi
la chaîne stéréo	hi-fi
la cheminée	fireplace
le fauteuil	armchair
le lecteur de CD(s)	CD player
le magnétophone à cassettes	cassette recorder
le magnétoscope	video recorder
la peinture	painting
la radio	radio
le tableau	painting
la télé(vision)	TV
le tourne-disque	record player

Tip CD is pronounced 'cédé' in French.

The dining room

la salle à manger	dining room
le buffet	sideboard
la chaise	chair
la table	table

The bathroom

la salle de bain(s)	the bathroom
la baignoire	bath(tub)
le bidet	bidet
la brosse à dents	toothbrush
les ciseaux (m)	scissors
le dentifrice	toothpaste
la douche	shower
le gant de toilette	flannel
le lavabo	hand basin
le miroir	mirror
le peigne	comb
la poudre	powder
le rasoir	razor
le robinet	tap
le savon	soap
la serviette	towel
le shampooing	shampoo

The bedroom

la chambre	the bedroom
l'armoire (f)	wardrobe
la commode	chest of drawers
la couette	duvet
la couverture	blanket
le drap	sheet
l'étagère (f)	shelf
le lit	bed
le manteau	blanket
l'ordinateur (m)	computer
l'oreiller (m)	pillow
le réveil	alarm clock
le tiroir	drawer

Everyday life
Home life

VOCABULARY

For more help see Success Guide page **11**

The kitchen

la cuisine	the kitchen
la casserole	saucepan
le congélateur	freezer
la cuisinière à gaz	gas cooker
la cuisinière électrique	electric cooker
l'évier (m)	sink
faire la cuisine	to cook
la farine	flour
le four à micro-ondes	microwave oven
le frigidaire	fridge
le frigo	fridge
le lave-vaisselle	dishwasher
la machine à laver	washing machine
la nourriture	food
le plateau	tray
le poêle	stove
la poêle	frying pan
le pot	pot
les provisions (f)	food
le tire-bouchon	corkscrew

The garden

le jardin	the garden
l'arbre (m)	tree
la barrière	gate/fence
la branche	branch
la feuille	leaf
la fleur	flower
la haie	hedge
le fruit	fruit
l'herbe (f)	grass
le mur	wall
la pelouse	lawn
la plante	plant

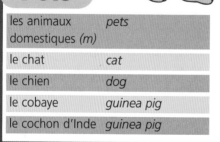

Pets

les animaux domestiques (m)	pets	le hamster	hamster
le chat	cat	le perroquet	parrot
le chien	dog	la perruche	budgerigar
le cobaye	guinea pig	le poisson	fish
le cochon d'Inde	guinea pig	le poisson rouge	goldfish
		la souris	mouse

Housework

le ménage	*housework*
débarrasser la table	*to clear the table*
faire la lessive	*to do the laundry/washing*
faire le jardinage	*to do the gardening*
faire le lit	*to make your bed*
faire le ménage	*to do the housework*
faire le repassage	*to do the ironing*
faire la vaisselle	*to do the washing up*
laver la voiture	*to wash the car*
laver le linge	*to do the laundry/washing*
mettre la table	*to lay the table*
mettre le couvert	*to lay the table*
le nettoyage à sec	*dry cleaning*
nettoyer	*to clean*
passer l'aspirateur *(m)*	*to vacuum*
la poussière	*dust*
la plume	*feather*
ranger sa chambre	*to tidy your room*
remplir le lave-vaisselle	*to load the dishwasher*
sécher	*to dry*
la tache	*stain*
le tas	*heap/pile*
le torchon	*tea cloth/tea towel*
vider le lave-vaisselle	*to empty the dishwasher*

Tip Use these words in the speaking test if asked: *Aidez-vous à la maison?*

Materials

les matériaux (m)	materials
le bois	wood
en bois	made of wood/wooden
le carton	cardboard
le coton	cotton
en coton	made of cotton/cotton
le cuir	leather
le feutre	felt
la laine	wool
en laine	made of wool/woollen
la matière plastique	plastic
en plastique	made of plastic/plastic
le métal	metal
en métal	made of metal/metal
le nylon	nylon
le papier	paper
le suède	suede

Verbs

aider	to help
arroser	to water
se brosser les dents	to brush your teeth
construire	to build
se coucher	to go to bed
coudre	to sew
se déshabiller	to get undressed
s'endormir	to go to sleep
fermer	to close
s'habiller	to get dressed
se laver	to have a wash/get washed
se lever	to get up
manger	to eat
se peigner	to comb your hair
prendre un bain	to have a bath
se raser	to shave
se réveiller	to wake up
stationner	to park
travailler	to work
utiliser	to use
vérifier	to check

Adjectives

ancien (ancienne)	former/ancient	électrique	electric
cassé(e)	broken	moderne	modern
clair(e)	clear/light	mou (molle)	soft
confortable	comfortable	neuf (neuve)	new
différent(e)	different	pittoresque	picturesque
dur(e)	hard	typique	typical

For more help see Success Guide pages 9 & 17

School

Subjects

les matières (f)	subjects	la géographie	geography
l'allemand (m)	German	la gymnastique	gymnastics
l'anglais (m)	English	l'histoire (f)	history
l'art (m)	art	l'informatique (f)	computing
la biologie	biology	les langues modernes (f)	modern languages
la chimie	chemistry		
le commerce	business studies	le latin	Latin
le dessin	drawing	les math(s) (f)	maths
l'éducation physique (f)	physical education	les mathématiques (f)	mathematics
		la physique	physics
l'EMT (éducation manuelle et technique) (f)	CDT	la science	science
		les sciences économiques (f)	economics
l'EPS (éducation physique et sportive) (f)	PE	les sciences naturelles (f)	biology
		la technologie	technology
l'espagnol (m)	Spanish	les travaux manuels (m)	handicraft
le français	French		

Model answers

Quelle matière préférez-vous?

You could well be asked this question in your speaking test. Your grade will depend on how ambitious and detailed your answer is.

J'aime les maths. `grade C`

J'aime bien les maths parce que le professeur est intéressant. `grade B`

J'aime bien les maths, parce que le professeur est intéressant, mais je préfère l'histoire, parce que je trouve que le travail qu'on fait nous prépare pour l'examen. `grade A`

J'aime bien les maths, parce que le professeur rend les cours toujours intéressants. Cependant je préfère l'histoire, parce que je trouve que le travail qu'on fait nous prépare pour l'examen. `grade A*`

In school

l'accent (m)	accent		la faute	fault/mistake
l'alphabet (m)	alphabet		les grandes vacances (f)	summer holidays
le bac(calauréat)	A-levels		l'horaire (f)	timetable
le bulletin	school report		les instructions (f)	instructions
le cercle	circle		la leçon	lesson
le chiffre	figure (numerical)		la ligne	line
la classe	class		la matière	subject
la description	description		le mot	word
les devoirs (m)	homework		la pause de midi	lunchtime
le diplôme	certificate		la phrase	sentence
l'échange (m)	exchange		le progrès	progress
l'emploi du temps (m)	timetable		la question	question
en sixième	in Year 7		la récréation	break
l'épreuve (f)	test		la rentrée	start of school year
l'erreur (f)	mistake		le silence	silence
l'examen (m)	examination		le succès	success
l'exemple (m)	example		le tableau noir	blackboard
par exemple	for example		la terminale	upper sixth
l'extrait (m)	extract		le trimestre	term

People

le/la concierge	caretaker
le directeur/la directrice	headmaster/-mistress
l'élève (m/f)	pupil
l'enseignant (m)/l'enseignante (f)	teacher
l'instituteur (m)/l'institutrice (f)	teacher (primary school)
le maître/la maîtresse	master/mistress
le professeur	teacher
le/la secrétaire	secretary
le surveillant/la surveillante	supervisor

Places

la cantine	canteen
le CES (Collège d'Enseignement Secondaire)	secondary school
le collège	school (secondary)
le couloir	corridor
la cour	school yard
l'école (f)	school (primary)
le gymnase	gym
le laboratoire	laboratory
le lycée	school (secondary)
la salle	room
la salle de classe	classroom
la salle de musique	music room
la salle des professeurs	staff room

Equipment

le matériel	equipment
le bic	ballpoint/biro
le cahier	exercise book
la calculatrice	calculator
le carnet	notebook
le cartable	school bag
le crayon	pencil
la gomme	rubber
la règle	rule/ruler
le stylo	pen
l'uniforme scolaire (m)	school uniform

Adjectives

absent(e)	absent	mixte	mixed
difficile	difficult	primaire	primary
facile	easy	privé(e)	private
faux (fausse)	false/wrong	scolaire	school
intéressant(e)	interesting	secondaire	secondary
inutile	useless	utile	useful
juste	correct	vrai(e)	true

Model answer

Décrivez votre collège.

Be ready for this question. To get an A* you must give a detailed answer involving an opinion and a justification.

A mon avis, mon collège est le meilleur de la ville **parce qu**'on vient d'installer des ordinateurs neufs dans chaque salle de classe.
In my opinion, my school is the best in the city because we have just had new computers installed in every classroom.

Role-play

Your friend is asking you about school.
1 Say your favourite subject is French.
2 Say you do not like your maths teacher.
3 Say you go home for lunch.
4 Say you live a kilometre away from school.
5 Say you come to school by bus.
6 !

EXAMINER'S ROLE AND SUGGESTED ANSWERS

Examiner Je vais te poser des questions sur ton collège. Et tes matières?

Candidate Ma matière préférée est le français.

Examiner Et les professeurs?

Candidate Je n'aime pas mon professeur de maths.

Examiner A midi tu manges un sandwich?

Candidate Non, je rentre chez moi.

Examiner Tu habites loin du collège?

Candidate J'habite à un kilomètre du collège.

Examiner Tu vas au collège à pied?

Candidate Non, j'y vais en bus.

Examiner Vous avez combien de cours par jour?

Candidate Cinq.

Tip Be ready for the unprepared question. Some boards indicate it on the role-play card by an exclamation mark and other boards by the instruction 'Be prepared to answer a question'. When the examiner (your teacher) asks you the unprepared question, listen carefully, paying particular attention to the question word. Here, it's *combien*. Make sure you know all the question words on page 9.

Food and drink

Meals

les repas (m)	meals
le déjeuner	lunch
le dessert	dessert
le dîner	dinner
l'entrée (f)	starter
le goûter	afternoon snack
le petit déjeuner	breakfast
le pique-nique	picnic
le plat	dish
le plat principal	main course
le souper	supper

Tip These words are often tested in the listening and reading tests.

Vegetables

les légumes (m)	vegetables
l'artichaut (m)	artichoke
la betterave	beetroot
la carotte	carrot
le champignon	mushroom
le chou	cabbage
le chou de Bruxelles	sprout
le chou-fleur	cauliflower
la courgette	courgette
le haricot vert	green bean/french bean
la laitue	lettuce
l'oignon (m)	onion
le petit pois	pea
la pomme de terre	potato
le riz	rice
la salade	salad/lettuce
la tomate	tomato

Fruit

les fruits (m)	fruit	le melon	melon
l'abricot (m)	apricot	mûr(e)	ripe
l'ananas (m)	pineapple	l'orange (f)	orange
la banane	banana	le pamplemousse	grapefruit
le cassis	blackcurrant	la pêche	peach
la cerise	cherry	la poire	pear
le citron	lemon	la pomme	apple
la fraise	strawberry	la prune	plum
la framboise	raspberry	le raisin	grape

For more help see Success Guide page 66

19

Meat

les viandes (f)	meat
l'agneau (m)	lamb
le bifteck	steak
le bœuf	beef
le canard	duck
la côtelette	chop
l'entrecôte (f)	rib steak
le jambon	ham
le lapin	rabbit
la merguez	spicy sausage
le mouton	mutton
le porc	pork
le poulet	chicken
le rôti	roast meat
le salami	salami
la saucisse	sausage
le saucisson	salami-type sausage
le steak	steak
le veau	veal

Seafood

les fruits de mer (m)	seafood
le coquillage	shellfish
le crabe	crab
de la mer/rivière	from the sea/river
les moules (f)	mussels
le poisson	fish
la sardine	sardine
le saumon	salmon
le thon	tuna
la truite	trout

Tip If asked for your opinion about France in your speaking test, you could mention French food. Use as many of these food and drink words as you can.

Breakfast

le petit déjeuner	breakfast
la baguette	loaf
le beurre	butter
les céréales (f)	cereal(s)
la confiture	jam
le croissant	croissant
le miel	honey
l'œuf (m)	egg
l'œuf à la coque (m)	boiled egg
le pain	bread
le pain grillé	toast
le toast	toast

Snacks

les snacks (m)	snacks
le biscuit	biscuit
le bonbon	sweet
les chips (m)	crisps
le chocolat	chocolate
le croque-madame	toasted cheese sandwich with chicken
le croque-monsieur	toasted cheese sandwich with ham
les frites (f)	chips
la glace	ice cream
l'omelette (f)	omelette
les pâtes (f)	pasta
la pizza	pizza
le sandwich	sandwich
les spaghetti (m)	spaghetti
la tarte	cake
la tartine	slice of bread and butter

Drinks

les boissons (f)	drinks
l'alcool (m)	alcohol
l'apéritif (m)	pre-dinner drink
la bière	beer
le café	coffee
le café-crème	white coffee
le chocolat chaud	hot chocolate
le cidre	cider
le citron pressé	freshly squeezed lemon
le coca	cola
l'eau (f)	water
l'eau minérale (f)	mineral water
le jus	juice
le jus de fruit	fruit juice
le lait	milk
la limonade	lemonade
l'Orangina (f)	orangeade
le sirop	cordial
la soif	thirst
le thé	tea
le thé au lait	tea with milk
le vin	wine

For more help see
Success Guide page **67**

Everyday life / Food and drink

Starters

l'entrée (f)	starters
les crudités (f)	raw vegetables
le hors-d'œuvre	starter
le pâté	pâté
le potage	soup
la soupe	soup

On the table

l'assiette (f)	plate
le bol	bowl
la cafetière	coffee pot
la carafe	carafe
le couteau	knife
la cuiller/la cuillère	spoon
la fourchette	fork
l'huile (f)	oil
la mayonnaise	mayonnaise
la moutarde	mustard
la nappe	tablecloth
le poivre	pepper
la sauce	gravy/sauce
le sel	salt
la serviette	napkin
servir	to serve
la soucoupe	saucer
le sucre	sugar
la table	table
la tasse	cup
le verre	glass
verser	to pour
le vinaigre	vinegar

Desserts

les desserts (m)	desserts
la crème (Chantilly)	(whipped) cream
la crêpe	pancake
le fromage	cheese
le gâteau	cake
la glace au chocolat/à la vanille	chocolate/vanilla ice cream
la pâtisserie	pastry
la tarte maison	home-made tart
le yaourt	yogurt

VOCABULARY

22

In the restaurant

à la carte	not from the set menu
l'addition (f)	bill (in a restaurant)
l'assiette (f)	plate
bon appétit	enjoy your meal
le bouchon	cork
la bouteille	bottle
le choix	choice
le couvert	place at table
la crêperie	pancake restaurant
l'escargot (m)	snail
le garçon	waiter
le menu (à 20 euros)	set (20-euro) menu
le patron/la patronne	restaurant owner
le plat du jour	today's special
les pommes vapeur (f)	steamed potatoes
le pourboire	tip
la recette	recipe
le restaurant	restaurant
le self	self-service restaurant
le serveur	waiter
la serveuse	waitress
le service non compris	service not included
la spécialité	speciality
les toilettes (f)	toilets
le végétarien/ la végétarienne	vegetarian

In the café

le café	café
le comptoir	counter
le garçon de café	waiter
la note	bill
l'ombre (f)	shade
la serveuse	waitress
le tarif	price list
la terrasse	terrace

For more help see Success Guide page 67

Role-play

IN THE GROCERY STORE

You are buying food and drink.

1 Ask for ham.
2 Ask for 200 grams.
3 Ask for beer.
4 Ask for a kilo of apples.
5 Ask how much it costs.

EXAMINER'S ROLE AND SUGGESTED ANSWERS

Examiner	Madame/Monsieur?
Candidate	Du jambon, s'il vous plaît.
Examiner	Combien, s'il vous plaît?
Candidate	Deux cents grammes.
Examiner	Avec ça?
Candidate	Une bouteille de bière, s'il vous plaît.
Examiner	Voilà.
Candidate	Et un kilo de pommes, s'il vous plaît.
Examiner	C'est tout?
Candidate	Oui, c'est combien?
Examiner	Cinq euros, madame/monsieur.

Model answer

At higher tier, the tasks will be much harder than these. For example:

Order a meal.

This is a common task. You must be prepared for it: work out before the exam what you are going to order.

Pour commencer, je voudrais une soupe aux tomates. Pour le plat principal, je voudrais un steak-frites. Comme dessert, je voudrais de la glace au chocolat. Et de l'eau minérale, s'il vous plaît.

Health and fitness

Sports

les sports (m)	sports	la natation	swimming
l'alpinisme (m)	climbing	la pêche	fishing
l'athlétisme (m)	athletics	la planche à roulettes	skateboarding
le basket	basketball	la planche à voile	windsurfing
le cyclisme	cycling	le rugby	rugby
l'équitation (f)	horse-riding	le ski nautique	water-skiing
faire du cheval	to go riding	les sports d'hiver (m)	winter sports
le football	football	le tennis	tennis
le handball	handball	la voile	sailing
le hockey	hockey	le volley	volleyball

Verbs

aimer	to like/to love	s'intéresser à	to be interested in
aimer bien	to quite like	jeter	to throw
améliorer	to improve	jouer au football	to play football
s'arrêter	to stop	lancer	to throw
assister à	to be present at	manquer	to miss (a goal)
attraper	to catch	marquer	to score (a goal)
choisir	to choose	mener	to lead
commencer	to begin	nager	to swim
courir	to run	patiner	to skate
se disputer	to argue/to quarrel	pêcher	to fish
empêcher	to prevent	perdre	to lose
envoyer	to send	ralentir	to slow down
finir	to finish	sauter	to jump
gagner	to win	siffler	to whistle
garder	to keep	terminer	to finish

For more help see Success Guide page 35

Nouns

la balle	ball (e.g. tennis)		l'étape (f)	stage
le ballon	ball (e.g. football)		le joueur	player
le but	goal		le match	match
le casque	helmet		le match nul	draw
le champion	champion		le résultat	result
le concours	competition		la mi-temps	half-time
le coup de pied	kick		le spectateur	spectator
le/la cycliste	cyclist		le terrain	pitch
l'équipe (f)	team			

Health problems

aller mal	to be unwell		se couper	to cut yourself
l'ampoule (f)	blister		la douleur	pain
avoir le mal de mer	to be seasick		être enrhumé(e)	to have a cold
avoir mal à l'estomac	to have stomach pains		se faire mal	to hurt yourself
avoir mal à l'oreille	to have earache		la fièvre	fever/temperature
avoir mal à la gorge	to have a sore throat		la grippe	flu
			être malade	to be sick/ill
avoir mal à la tête	to have a headache		la maladie	illness/ailment
			mourir	to die
avoir mal au cœur	to feel sick		piquer	to sting
avoir mal au dos	to have a sore back/backache		la piqûre	sting
			respirer	to breathe
avoir mal au ventre	to have a stomach ache		le rhume	cold
			se sentir	to feel
avoir mal aux dents	to have toothache		souffrir	to suffer/feel ill
se blesser	to hurt yourself		tomber malade	to fall ill
se casser (la jambe)	to break (your leg)		tousser	to cough
			trembler	to shiver
le coup de soleil	sunstroke		vomir	to vomit

For more help see Success Guide page **74**

The body

le corps	the body	la lèvre	lip
la bouche	mouth	la main	hand
le bras	arm	le menton	chin
les cheveux (m)	hair	le nez	nose
le cœur	heart	l'œil (m)	eye
le cou	neck	l'oreille (f)	ear
la coude	elbow	l'os (m)	bone
la dent	tooth	la peau	skin
le doigt	finger	le pied	foot
le dos	back	le poing	fist
l'épaule (f)	shoulder	la poitrine	breast/chest
l'estomac (m)	stomach	le sang	blood
la figure	face	le talon	heel
le genou	knee	la tête	head
la gorge	throat	le ventre	stomach
la jambe	leg	le visage	face
la joue	cheek	la voix	voice
la langue	tongue	les yeux (m)	eyes

Treatment

l'ambulance (f)	ambulance	l'ordonnance (f)	prescription
l'aspirine (f)	aspirin	la pilule	pill
le comprimé	tablet	prendre rendez-vous	to make an appointment
en forme	in good shape		
garder le lit	to stay in bed	le remède	remedy
guérir	to cure/get better	la santé	health
la médecine	medicine (the science)	le sparadrap	sticking plaster
le médicament	medicine (medication)		

Clothing

Clothes

les vêtements *(m)*	*clothes*	la mode	*fashion*
le blouson	*jacket*	le pantalon	*pair of trousers*
le bouton	*button*	le pardessus	*overcoat*
la chemise	*shirt*	le pull(over)	*pullover*
la chemise de nuit	*nightdress*	le pyjama	*pyjamas*
le chemisier	*blouse*	la robe	*dress*
le collant	*tights*	le short	*shorts*
le complet	*suit (man's)*	le slip	*briefs*
le costume	*suit (man's)*	le slip de bain	*swimming trunks*
la cravate	*tie*	le soutien-gorge	*bra*
la culotte	*knickers*	le survêtement	*tracksuit*
l'écharpe *(f)*	*scarf (neck)*	la taille	*size (clothes)*
le foulard	*scarf (head)*	le T-shirt	*T-shirt*
l'imperméable *(m)*	*raincoat*	le tailleur	*suit (woman's)*
le jean	*jeans*	le tricot	*sweater*
la jupe	*skirt*	la veste	*jacket*
le maillot de bain	*swimming costume*		

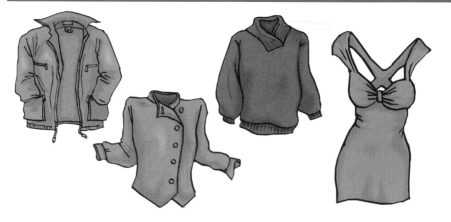

For more help see **Success Guide** page **71**

Accessories

l'argent (m)	silver	le maquillage	make-up
la bague	ring	la montre	watch
la boucle d'oreille	earring	l'or (m)	gold
la ceinture	belt	le parapluie	umbrella
le chapeau	hat	le portefeuille	wallet
le collier	necklace	le porte-monnaie	purse
le gant	glove	le rouge à lèvres	lipstick
le képi	kepi	le sac à main	handbag
les lunettes (f)	glasses		

Hyphenated nouns are nearly always masculine.

Footwear

la basket	trainer
la botte	boot
la chaussette	sock
la chaussure	shoe
la paire	pair
la pantoufle	slipper
la pointure	size (shoes)
la sandale	sandal
le soulier	shoe

Family and friends

Family

la famille	family
l'adulte (m/f)	adult
l'âge (m)	age
aîné(e)	older/oldest
le beau-frère	brother-in-law
le beau-père	father-in-law
le bébé	baby
la belle-mère	mother-in-law
la belle-sœur	sister-in-law
cadet (cadette)	younger/youngest
célibataire	single (not married)
le cousin/ la cousine	cousin
la dame	lady
le demi-frère	half-brother
la demi-sœur	half-sister
divorcé(e)	divorced
l'enfant (m/f)	child
l'épouse (f)	wife
l'époux (m)	husband
la femme	wife/woman
le fiancé/ la fiancée	fiancé
la fille	girl/daughter
le fils	son
le frère	brother
le garçon	boy
le/la gosse	child/kid
la grand-mère	grandmother
le grand-parent	grandparent
le grand-père	grandfather
l'homme (m)	man
le jumeau/ la jumelle	twin
maman	Mummy
le mari	husband
marié(e)	married
les membres de la famille (m)	family members
la mère	mother
mourir	to die
naître	to be born
le neveu	nephew
la nièce	niece
l'oncle (m)	uncle
papa	Dad
les parents (m)	parents
le père	father
le petit-fils	grandson
la petite-fille	grand-daughter
les petits-enfants (m)	grandchildren
la sœur	sister
la tante	aunt
le veuf	widower
la veuve	widow
vivre	to live

Friends

l'ami (m)/l'amie (f)	friend
l'amour (m)	love
beaucoup de monde	a lot of people
la bise	kiss (on cheek)
le/la camarade	friend
le copain/ la copine	friend
la correspondance	mail
le correspondant/ la correspondante	penfriend
de la part de	from
le dialogue	conversation
les gens (m)	people
l'hospitalité (f)	hospitality
l'invitation (f)	invitation
le jumelage	twinning
jumelé(e)	twinned
la lettre	letter
le mensonge	lie
les nouvelles (f)	news
la personne	person
le rendez-vous	meeting
la réponse	reply
la surprise	surprise
la surprise-partie	party
tout le monde	everybody
la ville jumelée	twin town
le visiteur	visitor
les vœux (m)	wishes

Model answer

Describe a member of your family.

If asked to do this in the speaking test, give a long answer that shows your knowledge of vocabulary and structure.

Je vais décrire ma sœur, parce que je m'entends bien avec elle. Elle est toujours célibataire, mais elle a un fiancé. Elle est vraiment belle: elle a de beaux cheveux longs et frisés et les yeux bleu clair. Quand elle sort avec son fiancé, elle porte toujours des boucles d'oreille et un collier. Aujourd'hui, elle porte un chemisier en soie et une jupe bleu marine avec des chaussures en cuir – bleu marine aussi, bien sûr!

Verbs

aimer	to like/love
aimer bien	to quite like
s'allonger	to lie down
s'amuser	to have a good time
s'asseoir	to sit down
bavarder	to chatter
chanter	to sing
correspondre	to correspond
danser	to dance
se débrouiller	to sort out your difficulties/ to manage
se dépêcher	to hurry
se détendre	to relax
se disputer	to argue/to quarrel
s'écrire	to write to each other
s'ennuyer	to be bored
s'entendre avec	to get on well with
épouser	to marry
se fâcher	to get angry
faire des photos	to take photos
faire des promenades	to go for walks
faire du babysitting	to babysit
faire la connaissance de	to get to know
faire les courses	to go shopping
faire partie de	to be a part of/ to belong to
s'intéresser à	to be interested in
inviter	to invite
jouer	to play
manquer (il me manque)	to be lacking (I miss him)
se moquer de	to make fun of
oublier	to forget
pardonner	to forgive
parler	to talk
partir	to leave
pleurer	to cry
présenter	to introduce
se promener	to go for a walk
punir	to punish
raconter	to tell
recevoir	to receive
se rencontrer	to meet (each other)
rendre visite à	to visit (a person)
rentrer	to go home
se reposer	to rest
voir	to see
se voir	to see each other

For more help see Success Guide page 71

Personal characteristics

Positive adjectives

accueillant(e)	welcoming		intéressant(e)	interesting
affectueux (-euse)	affectionate		magnifique	magnificent
aimable	pleasant		meilleur(e)	better/best
amusant(e)	funny		merveilleux (-euse)	marvellous
avantageux (-euse)	advantageous		mignon (mignonne)	nice/sweet
bon (bonne)	good		optimiste	optimistic
calme	quiet		riche	rich
célèbre	famous		parfait(e)	perfect
charmant(e)	charming		passionnant(e)	exciting
cher (chère)	dear		poli(e)	polite
chic	elegant		positif (-ive)	positive
comique	funny		pratique	practical
compliqué(e)	complicated		précis(e)	accurate
correct(e)	correct/proper		préféré(e)	favourite
au courant	well informed		propre	clean
drôle	funny		sage	well behaved/wise
dynamique	dynamic		sain(e)	healthy
élégant(e)	elegant		sensass	sensational
étonnant(e)	astonishing		spécial(e)	special
excellent(e)	excellent		sportif (sportive)	sporting
extraordinaire	extraordinary		sympa(thique)	nice/friendly
favori (favorite)	favourite		tranquille	quiet/calm
formidable	tremendous/great		unique	unique
génial(e)	excellent			
gentil (gentille)	nice			
honnête	honest			
important(e)	important			
impressionnant(e)	impressive			
intelligent(e)	intelligent			

Some informal and shortened adjectives, e.g. *chic*, *sensass* and *sympa*, don't change in the feminine or plural.

Negative adjectives

affreux (-euse)	*awful*	malheureux (-euse)	*unhappy/ unfortunate*
bête	*silly/stupid*	mauvais(e)	*bad*
bruyant(e)	*noisy*	méchant(e)	*naughty*
dangereux (-euse)	*dangerous*	moche	*ugly*
désagréable	*unpleasant*	mystérieux (-euse)	*mysterious*
difficile	*difficult*	négatif (-ive)	*negative*
égoïste	*selfish*	paresseux (-euse)	*lazy*
ennuyeux (-euse)	*boring*	pauvre	*poor*
fatigant(e)	*tiring*	pire	*worse/worst*
fou (folle)	*mad*	sale	*dirty*
grave	*serious*	sérieux (-euse)	*serious*
horrible	*horrible*	sévère	*strict/severe*
idiot(e)	*silly*	silencieux (-euse)	*silent*
impoli(e)	*impolite*	timide	*shy*
impossible	*impossible*	vilain (vilaine)	*naughty*
laid(e)	*ugly*		

Physical descriptions

âgé(e)	*aged/elderly*	joli(e)	*pretty/attractive*
aveugle	*blind*	lisse	*straight*
beau (belle)	*beautiful*	maigre	*thin*
bien habillé(e)	*well dressed*	mince	*thin/slim*
bouclé(e)	*curly*	ondulé(e)	*wavy*
d'âge moyen	*middle-aged*	petit(e)	*short/small*
faible	*weak*	sourd(e)	*deaf*
frisé(e)	*curly*		
grand(e)	*tall/large*		
gras (grasse)	*fat*		
jeune	*young*		

Tip You are often asked in the speaking test: *Décrivez votre famille*. Use the family words on page 30 with the words on these pages.

Free time

le bal	dance		la location	hiring out/ renting out
les boules (f)	bowls		les loisirs (m)	free time/leisure
la boum	party		le magnétophone à cassettes	cassette recorder
le bricolage	model-making/DIY		les mots croisés (m)	crossword
la canne à pêche	fishing rod		la natation	swimming
la cassette	cassette		le passe-temps	hobby
le CD	CD player/CD		le patin (à roulettes)	(roller) skate
la chaîne hi-fi	hi-fi		la pêche	fishing
la chaîne stéréo	hi-fi		la peinture	painting
le championnat	championship		la pièce de théâtre	play
la chance	luck		la piste	track/ski slope
la chanson	song		la planche à voile	surfboard
le chanteur/ la chanteuse	singer		la poupée	doll
la chose	thing		la promenade	walk
la cigarette	cigarette		la randonnée	long walk/hike
le cirque	circus		le sac à dos	rucksack
le disc compact	compact disc		le spectacle	show
le disque	record		le sport	sport
la distraction	entertainment		la télévision par cable	cable (TV)
les échecs (m)	chess		le vélo	bike
l'exposition (f)	exhibition		la voile	sailing
la fête	party		le VTT (vélo tout terrain)	mountain bike
le jardinage	gardening		le week-end	weekend
le jeu	game		le yoga	yoga
le jeu d'arcade	arcade game			
le jeu électronique	computer game			
le jeu vidéo	video game			
le jouet	toy			

Places

le bar	bar
le bistrot	bar/pub
la boîte de nuit	night club
le café	café
le café-tabac	café/tobacconist's
le centre de loisirs	leisure centre
le centre sportif	sports centre
le cinéma	cinema
le club	club
la disco(thèque)	disco
le jardin zoologique	zoo
la maison des jeunes	youth club
la patinoire	ice-skating rink
le stade	stadium
le théâtre	theatre

Reading

la lecture	reading
la bande dessinée	comic strip
illustré(e)	illustrated
le journal	newspaper
lire	to read
le livre	book
le magazine	magazine
la page	page
la revue	magazine
le roman	novel
le roman d'amour	romantic novel
le roman policier	detective novel

At the cinema

l'acteur (m)/ l'actrice (f)	actor
la comédie	comedy
le commencement	start
le début	beginning
le dessin animé	cartoon
le film comique	comedy film
le film d'amour	romantic film
le film d'aventures	adventure film
le film d'épouvante	horror film
le film d'horreur	horror film
le film policier	detective film
le film de science-fiction	science-fiction film
la fin	end

Tip Use the words on these pages and the verbs on page 38 to answer the common speaking test question *Qu'est-ce que vous aimez faire?*

l'ouvreuse (f)	usherette
le rang	row
la séance	performance
sous-titré	subtitled
la vedette	star
en version française	dubbed in French
en version originale	not dubbed
le western	western film

TV and radio

les actualités *(f)*	news
la cassette vidéo	video cassette
la chaîne (de télévision)	(TV) channel
le DVD	DVD
l'écran *(m)*	screen
l'émission *(f)*	programme/ broadcast
en différé	not live
en direct	live
le feuilleton	soap
l'image *(f)*	picture
les informations *(f)*	news
le journal télévisé	TV news
le lecteur de DVD(s)	DVD player
le magnétoscope	video recorder
le programme	schedule
la radio	radio
le satellite	satellite
la télé	TV
le téléspectateur	viewer
le téléviseur	TV set
la télévision	televison

Tip DVD is pronounced 'dévédé'.

Music

la musique	music
la batterie	percussion/drums
la clarinette	clarinet
classique	classical
le concert	concert
la flûte à bec	recorder
la guitare	guitar
la hi-fi	hi-fi
l'instrument de musique *(m)*	musical instrument
le jazz	jazz
jouer du piano	to play the piano
le musicien *(m)/* la musicienne *(f)*	musician
la musique classique	classical music
l'opéra *(m)*	opera
l'orchestre *(m)*	orchestra
le piano	piano
le pop	pop
le rock	rock
le son	sound
le studio	studio
la trompette	trumpet
la trousse	instrument case
le violon	violin

For more help see **Success Guide** pages **34–35**

Verbs

accompagner	to accompany	faire une promenade	to go for a walk
acheter	to buy	faire une randonnée	to go for a long walk/hike
aimer	to like/love		
s'amuser	to have a good time	fumer	to smoke
se baigner	to bathe	jouer aux cartes	to play cards
bavarder	to chatter	jouer de la musique	to play music
bricoler	to make models/ do DIY		
se bronzer	to sunbathe	manger	to eat
chanter	to sing	marcher	to walk
dessiner	to draw	nager	to swim
se détendre	to relax	parler	to talk
économiser	to save (money)	patiner	to skate
écouter	to listen (to)	pêcher	to fish
faire des économies	to save money	rire	to laugh
		sauter	to jump
faire des promenades	to go for walks	sortir	to go out
faire du bricolage	to make models/ do DIY	visiter (un endroit)	to visit (a place)
		voyager	to travel
faire du lèche-vitrines	to go window shopping		

Model answer

Qu'est-ce que vous aimez faire? When asked this in the speaking test, most candidates start with **J'aime** and then give a list of hobbies: **le football**, **la lecture** etc. That is OK for grade C, but for A* you need to be more ambitious!

Ça dépend. Si j'ai de l'argent, j'adore aller au cinéma avec mes amis. Avant d'entrer dans le cinéma, on va dans un café et on bavarde et on discute. Je me passionne pour les films comiques, mais malheureusement mes amis ont des opinions différentes! Après avoir vu le film, on retourne au café pour discuter de ce qu'on vient de voir. Si je n'ai pas d'argent, je fais du lèche-vitrine et je fais des randonnées.

For types of film, see page 36.

VOCABULARY

Role-play

A friend phones you to ask what you want to do today.

1 Say you would like to go to the cinema.
2 Say there is an American film showing.
3 Say you will meet in front of the cinema.
4 Say you will meet at half past six.
5 Say you will go to the café afterwards.

EXAMINER'S ROLE AND SUGGESTED ANSWERS

Examiner	Je te téléphone pour voir ce qu'on va faire. Qu'est-ce qu'on fait aujourd'hui?
Candidate	Je veux aller au cinéma.
Examiner	Il y a un bon film?
Candidate	Il y a un film américain.
Examiner	Où est-ce qu'on se retrouve?
Candidate	Devant le cinéma.
Examiner	A quelle heure?
Candidate	A six heures et demie.
Examiner	Et après?
Candidate	On va au café.

Holidays

On holiday

l'appareil-photo (m)	camera	la N2 (Route Nationale 2)	(main road, equivalent of A2)
les arrhes (f)	deposit	le passager	passenger
l'arrivée (f)	arrival	le passeport	passport
au bord de la mer	at the seaside	la pellicule	film (for camera)
l'auto-stop (m)	hitch-hiking	la photo	photo
l'aventure (f)	adventure	le projet	plan
bon voyage!	have a good trip!	les renseignements (m)	information
bon week-end!	have a good weekend!	la réservation	reservation
la brochure	brochure	le retard	delay
le bureau de renseignements	information office	rien à déclarer	nothing to declare
le bureau de tourisme	tourist office	la saison	season
la carte	map	le séjour	stay
la colonie de vacances	holiday camp (for children)	le ski	skiing
le congé	time off/holiday	le souvenir	souvenir
déclarer	to declare	la station de ski	ski resort
le dépliant	leaflet	le syndicat d'initiative	tourist office
la douane	customs	le tour	tour
l'étranger (m)/ l'étrangère (f)	foreigner	le/la touriste	tourist
à l'étranger	abroad	le trajet	journey
l'excursion (f)	trip	les vacances (f)	holidays
le gîte	holiday let	en vacances	on holiday
le groupe	group	la valise	suitcase
le/la guide	guide	la visite	visit/trip
l'hébergement (m)	lodging	le voyage	journey
		le voyageur	traveller

Camping

l'accueil *(m)*	*welcome/reception*
l'allumette *(f)*	*match*
le bloc sanitaire	*toilet block*
le camp	*camp*
le campeur	*camper*
le camping	*campsite/camping*
le canif	*penknife*
la caravane	*caravan*
la corde	*rope*
l'eau non potable *(f)*	*non-drinking water*
l'eau potable *(f)*	*drinking water*
l'emplacement *(m)*	*pitch*
l'endroit *(m)*	*spot/place*
le feu	*fire*
la lampe à poche	*torch*
le matériel	*equipment*
le moustique	*mosquito*
l'ouvre-boîte *(m)*	*tin opener*
l'ouvre-bouteille *(m)*	*bottle opener*
la pile	*battery*
le plat cuisiné	*ready meal*
en plein air	*in the open air*
le sac de couchage	*sleeping bag*
la salle de jeux	*games room*
la tente	*tent*

At the hotel

l'ascenseur *(m)*	*lift*
l'auberge de jeunesse *(f)*	*youth hostel*
les bagages *(m)*	*luggage*
la chambre avec un grand lit	*room with a double bed*
la chambre de famille	*family room*
la chambre de libre	*room free*
la chambre pour deux personnes	*double room*
la chambre pour une personne	*single room*
la clé/clef	*key*
le domicile	*home/place of residence*
le dortoir	*dormitory*
en avance	*in advance*
la fiche	*form*
l'hôtel *(m)*	*hotel*
inclus(e)	*included*
libre	*free*
le message	*message*
la nationalité	*nationality*
né(e) le ...	*date of birth*
le nom	*name*
le nom de famille	*surname*
par jour	*per day*
par personne	*per person*
la pension (complète)	*full board*
le prénom	*first name*
la réception	*reception*
le règlement	*set of rules*
la vue	*view*

VOCABULARY

For more help see Success Guide pages 48–49

Verbs

accepter	to accept		faire des photos	to take photos
aller	to go		faire des promenades	to go for walks
s'en aller	to go away		faire du camping	to camp
s'allonger	to lie down		faire le plein	to fill up
arriver	to arrive		grimper	to climb
attendre	to wait for		jouer	to play
atterrir	to land (plane)		jouer au football	to play football
attirer	to attract		loger dans	to stay in
avoir envie de	to want to		louer	to hire
se baigner	to bathe		nager	to swim
boire	to drink		se noyer	to drown
se bronzer	to sunbathe		parler	to talk
changer (de chambre)	to change (rooms)		partir	to leave
comprendre	to understand		payer	to pay
conduire	to drive		pêcher	to fish
confirmer	to confirm		se promener	to go for a walk
connaître	to know (a person or place)		se renseigner	to get information
coûter	to cost		réserver	to book
danser	to dance		rester	to stay
décoller	to take off (plane)		retourner	to return
découvrir	to discover		revenir	to return
dépenser	to spend (money)		signer	to sign
donner sur	to overlook		sonner	to ring
dormir	to sleep		sortir	to go out
s'échapper	to escape		traverser	to cross
économiser	to save (money)		trouver	to find
s'ennuyer	to be bored		se trouver	to be located
envoyer	to send		venir	to come
faire des économies	to save money		visiter (un endroit)	to visit (a place)
			voir	to see
			voyager	to travel

Special events

Incidents

l'argent *(m)*	money
l'assurance *(f)*	insurance
au feu!	fire!
le cambriolage	burglary
le cambrioleur	burglar
les chèques de voyage *(m)*	travellers' cheques
la collision	collision
le danger	danger
disparu(e)	disappeared
l'explosion *(f)*	explosion
l'incendie *(m)*	fire
l'inondation *(f)*	flood
le meutre	murder
les objets trouvés *(m)*	lost property
le passeport	passport
perdre	to lose
la perte	loss
la pièce d'identité	ID
la police-secours	emergency services
la récompense	reward
le tremblement de terre	earthquake
le trésor	treasure
tuer	to kill
voler	to steal
le voleur	thief
le voyou	hooligan

Occasions

l'anniversaire *(m)*	birthday
bon anniversaire	happy birthday
bonne année	happy new year
la bûche de Noël	Christmas log
le cadeau	present
Dieu *(m)*	God
les félicitations *(f)*	congratulations
le jour férié	bank holiday
la Fête Nationale	Bastille Day (14th July)
fêter	to celebrate
le Jour de l'An	New Year's Day
joyeux Noël	happy Christmas
le mariage	wedding
le marié/la mariée	groom/bride
la messe	mass
la mort	death
la naissance	birth
les noces *(f)*	wedding
Noël *(m)*	Christmas
le Nouvel An	New Year
Pâques *(f)*	Easter
la Pentecôte	Whitsun
souhaiter	to wish
le Tour de France	Tour de France (cycle race)
la Toussaint	All Saints' Day (30th November)
la vendange	grape harvest

For more help see Success Guide pages 63, 74

Role-play

Situation: the notes and pictures below give an outline of the beginning of a holiday last year, when you, or someone you know, visited some friends in Switzerland.

This type of role-play is used by OCR for Higher Tier.

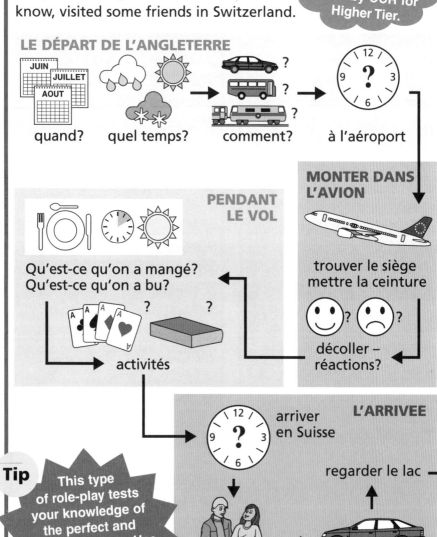

LE DÉPART DE L'ANGLETERRE

quand? quel temps? comment? à l'aéroport

MONTER DANS L'AVION

PENDANT LE VOL

Qu'est-ce qu'on a mangé?
Qu'est-ce qu'on a bu?

activités

trouver le siège
mettre la ceinture

décoller –
réactions?

L'ARRIVEE

arriver en Suisse

regarder le lac

rencontrer la famille – description

en route pour la maison traverser la ville de Genève

Tip This type of role-play tests your knowledge of the perfect and imperfect tenses. Use the imperfect when talking about the weather.

EXAMINER'S ROLE AND SUGGESTED ANSWERS

Candidate L'année dernière je suis parti(e) en vacances au mois de juin avec mes parents. Je voulais rendre visite à mes amis en Suisse.

Examiner Quel temps faisait-il?

Tip 'I wasn't frightened.' Good use of the imperfect.

Candidate Il faisait beau et nous sommes allés à l'aéroport en taxi. Nous sommes montés dans l'avion et j'ai trouvé un siège, j'ai mis ma ceinture et l'avion est parti. Je n'avais pas peur.

Examiner Qu'est-ce que tu as fait pendant le vol?

Candidate J'ai joué aux cartes et j'ai lu. Nous avons déjeuné, mais le repas n'était très bon. C'était du poulet, et je ne l'ai pas aimé. Mais j'ai bu du coca. Je suis arrivé(e) en Suisse à dix heures et mes amis m'attendaient a l'aéroport. Ils étaient très sympa. En route pour la maison nous avons traversé la ville de Genève, nous avons admiré le lac et plus tard nous sommes arrivés à la maison. Nous avons mangé un repas superbe et nous nous sommes couchés.

Examiner Et tes impressions?

Candidate Je pense que le voyage s'est très bien passé et que mes amis étaient très gentils.

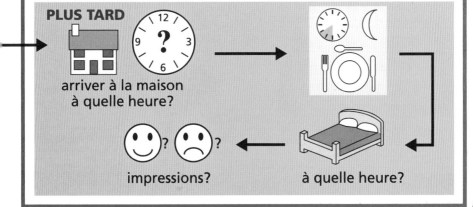

PLUS TARD

arriver à la maison à quelle heure?

impressions?

à quelle heure?

Role-play

You have had an accident at school during a French exchange visit and you are now at the hospital. Your teacher will play the part of the doctor.

1 Accident.
2 Où et quand?
3 Où avez-vous mal?
4 !

Tip If your exam board is OCR, you may well have to describe an incident for Role-play 3.

EXAMINER'S ROLE AND SUGGESTED ANSWERS

Examiner Qu'est-ce qui vous est arrivé?

Candidate J'ai eu un accident. J'ai glissé et je suis tombé(e).

Examiner Où exactement et quand?

Candidate A une heure de l'après-midi. J'étais sur un escalier et quelqu'un m'a poussé(e).

Examiner Vous avez mal où exactement?

Candidate J'ai mal au bras.

Examiner On va l'examiner. Vous êtes ici en vacances?

Candidate Non, je participe à un échange.

Tip Always read the preliminary instructions closely for clues to what the unprepared question will be. There's a good example of such a clue here.

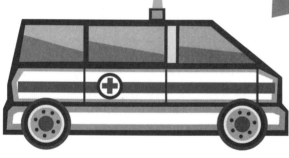

46

Local area

In the street

dans la rue	*in the street*
l'affiche *(f)*	*poster*
l'allée *(f)*	*path/avenue*
l'avenue *(f)*	*avenue*
le banc	*bench*
le boulevard	*avenue*
le bout	*end*
le bruit	*noise*
le carrefour	*crossroads*
la circulation	*traffic*
le code de la route	*highway code*
le coin	*corner*
défendu(e)	*forbidden*
devant	*in front of*
l'embouteillage *(m)*	*traffic jam*
le feu (rouge)	*traffic lights*
le flic *(slang)*	*policeman/cop*
l'HLM (habitation à loyer modéré) *(f)*	*council flat*
interdit(e)	*forbidden*

le kiosque	*kiosk/stand*
le kiosque à journaux	*news stand*
le mètre	*metre*
la mobylette	*small motorcycle*
le panneau	*(road) sign*
le passage à niveau	*level crossing*
le passage clouté	*pedestrian crossing*
le passant/ la passante	*passer-by*
le piéton	*pedestrian*
prière de ...	*please ...*
la queue	*queue*
le rond-point	*roundabout*
la rue	*street*
sens interdit	*no entry*
sens unique	*one way*
toutes directions	*all traffic*
le trottoir	*pavement*
la zone piétonne	*pedestrian zone*

Buildings

les bâtiments *(m)*	buildings	l'office du tourisme *(m)*	tourist office
la bibliothèque	library	la Poste	post office
la cathédrale	cathedral	le poste de police	police station
le centre commercial	shopping centre	la tour	tower
le château	castle		
le commissariat	police station		
l'église *(f)*	church		
la gendarmerie	police station		
l'hôpital *(m)*	hospital		
l'hôtel de ville *(m)*	town hall		
l'immeuble *(m)*	block of flats		
la mairie	town hall		
le monument	monument		
le musée	museum		

Be careful! La tour is a tower, but le tour is a tour.

In town

en ville	in town	le parc	park
la banlieue	outskirts (of a city)/suburbs	parisien (-ienne)	Parisian
le centre (historique)	(historic) centre	le parking	car park
		la piscine	swimming pool
le centre-ville	town centre	la place	square
la fontaine	fountain	le plan	map (of town)
l'habitant *(m)*/ l'habitante *(f)*	inhabitant	le pont	bridge
		le quartier	district
l'industrie *(f)*	industry	le village	village
le jardin public	park	la ville	town

Points of the compass

les points cardinaux *(m)*	*points of the compass*
l'est *(m)*	*east*
le nord	*north*
l'ouest *(m)*	*west*
le sud	*south*

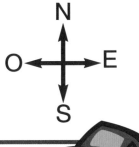

Tip

Make sure you know the difference between *droit* and *droite*. They are often tested in the listening test.

Directions

les directions *(f)*	*directions*
à … kilomètres	*… kilometres away*
à … mètres	*… metres away*
à … minutes	*… minutes away*
le côté	*side*
la droite	*right*
à droite	*to/on the right*
sur votre droite	*on your right*
en bas	*below/downstairs*
en haut	*above/upstairs*
entouré(e) de …	*surrounded by …*
en face de …	*opposite …*
la flèche	*arrow*
la gauche	*left*
à gauche	*to/on the left*
sur votre gauche	*on your left*
là	*there*
là-bas	*over there*
le long de …	*along …*
loin de …	*far from …*
loin d'ici	*far from here*
où?	*where?*
par ici	*this way*
par là	*that way*
partout	*everywhere*
pour aller à …?	*how do I get to …?*
près de …	*near …*
proche	*near*
tout droit	*straight on*

VOCABULARY

For more help see Success Guide pages 52–54

VOCABULARY

Role-play

You are in your local town and a French tourist asks you for directions to the bus station, which is two kilometres away.

1 Aider?
2 Transport?
3 Directions (deux détails)
4 !

EXAMINER'S ROLE AND SUGGESTED ANSWERS

Examiner   Pardon. Pouvez-vous m'aider? Où est la gare routière, s'il vous plaît?

Candidate   Oui, je peux vous aider. La gare routière est à deux kilomètres d'ici.

Examiner   Il y a des transports publics?

Candidate   Vous pouvez prendre un taxi ou un bus.

Examiner   J'irai à pied peut-être. C'est où exactement?

Candidate   Prenez cette rue. Allez tout droit et tournez à gauche au carrefour. La gare est sur votre droite.

Examiner   Vous parlez bien le français. Vous êtes de quelle nationalité?

Candidate   Je suis britannique.

Shops and services

Shops

les magasins (m)	shops		la crémerie	dairy
l'agence de voyages (f)	travel agent's		l'épicerie (f)	grocer's
l'alimentation (f)	grocer's		l'épicier/l'épicière	grocer
le boucher/ la bouchère	butcher		la librairie	book shop
la boucherie	butcher's		le libre-service	self-service
la boulangerie	baker's		le marchand de fruits et légumes	greengrocer
le boulanger/ la boulangère	baker		la papeterie	stationer's
la boutique	shop		la parfumerie	perfume shop
le bureau de poste	post office		la pâtisserie	cake shop
le bureau de tabac	tobacconist's		la pharmacie	chemist's
la charcuterie	pork butcher's/ delicatessen		le pharmacien/ la pharmacienne	chemist
la confiserie	sweet shop		la poissonnerie	fish shop
			la Poste	post office

Shopping

l'achat (m)	purchase		pas trop cher	not too expensive
l'argent (m)	money		le prix	price
l'article (m)	article/item		le prix fixe	set price
et avec ça?	anything else?		la promotion	special offer
c'est combien?	how much is it?		le rayon	department (in store)
c'est tout	that's all		le reçu	receipt
la cabine d'essayage	fitting room		la réduction	reduction
le chariot	(supermarket) trolley		réduit(e)	reduced
le client/la cliente	customer		le sac	bag
combien?	how much?/ how many?		les soldes (f)	sales
			la sorte	sort
l'étage (m)	floor, storey		une sorte de ...	a type of ...
fermé(e)	closed		au sous-sol (m)	in the basement
la fermeture	closing		le supermarché	supermarket
le gramme	gram		la taille	size/waist
le grand magasin	department store		la tranche	slice
gratuit(e)	free (of charge)		la TVA (taxe sur la valeur ajoutée)	VAT
l'hypermarché (f)	hypermarket		en vente	on sale
le kilo	kilo		la vitrine	shop window
la liste	list			
le magasin	shop			
le marché	market			
le morceau	piece			
ouvert(e)	open			
l'ouverture (f)	opening			
le panier	basket			
le parfum	perfume			
pas très cher	not very expensive			

Tip Asking 'How much is it?' is a very common task in role-play, and you will lose marks if you say just *Combien?* Say *C'est combien?*

Shopping verbs

acheter	to buy	faire du lèche-vitrines	to go window shopping
aller chercher	to fetch	faire les commissions	to do the shopping
attirer	to attract	faire les courses	to go shopping
changer	to change	garer	to park
commander	to order	livrer	to deliver
comparer	to compare	payer	to pay
conseiller	to advise/ recommend	prendre	to take
coûter	to cost	se renseigner	to get information
décrire	to describe	servir	to serve
demander	to ask	sonner	to ring
dépenser	to spend (money)	stationner	to park
désirer	to want	trouver	to find
entrer	to enter	vendre	to sell
essayer	to try		
éviter	to avoid		

At the post office

l'adresse (f)	address	la lettre par avion	airmail letter
la boîte aux lettres	post box/ letter box	la lettre recommandée	registered letter
la carte postale	postcard	mettre à la poste	to post
le code postal	post code	le paquet	packet/parcel
le colis	packet/parcel	par avion	by air
le courrier	mail	la Poste	post/post office
l'enveloppe (f)	envelope	la poste restante	poste restante
envoyer	to send	poster	to post
le facteur/ la factrice	postman/ -woman	le télégramme	telegram
fragile	fragile	le timbre (de 20 cents)	(20-cent) stamp
urgent(e)	urgent		

For more help see **Success Guide** pages **70** & **73**

At the bank

accepter	to accept		le cours (du dollar)	(dollar) exchange rate
l'argent (m)	money		le Crédit Agricole	(name of a bank)
l'argent de poche (m)	pocket money			
la banque	bank		échanger	to exchange
le billet (de 10 euros)	(10-euro) note		emprunter	to borrow
			encaisser	to cash
la BNP (Banque Nationale de Paris)	(name of a bank)		l'euro (m)	euro
			expliquer	to explain
le bureau de change	exchange office		fermer	to close
la caisse	cash point/till		le guichet	counter window
le carnet de chèques	cheque book		la livre sterling	pound sterling
la carte bancaire	banker's card		la monnaie	change
le cent/centime	cent		la pièce (de 10 cents)	(10-cent) coin
changer	to change			
le chèque	cheque		la pièce d'identité	ID
le chèque de voyage	traveller's cheque		prêter	to lend
			remplir une fiche	to fill in a form
le chéquier	cheque book		signer	to sign
la commission	commission		la somme	sum
le compte	account		le taux de change	exchange rate
compter	to count		transférer	to transfer

For more help see **Success Guide** pages **70** & **72**

Nature & environment

In the country

l'ambiance (f)	atmosphere
le bassin	pond
le bois	wood
la campagne	countryside
le champ	field
le chemin	path/way
la colline	hill
la côte	coast
l'étoile (f)	star
le fleuve	(large) river
la forêt	forest
l'herbe (f)	grass
l'île (f)	island
le lac	lake
la lune	moon
la mer	sea
le milieu naturel	the environment
le monde	world
la montagne	mountain
la nature	nature
le paysage	countryside/ scenery
la région	region
la rivière	(small) river
le sommet	top (e.g. of a hill)
la terre	earth
la vallée	valley
le voisin/ la voisine	neighbour

At the seaside

au bord de la mer	at the seaside
se baigner	to bathe
le bateau	boat
se bronzer	to sunbathe
la crème solaire	sun cream
la falaise	cliff
la marée (basse/haute)	(low/high) tide
nager	to swim
la plage	beach
plonger	to dive
le port	port
le rocher	rock
le sable	sand
la serviette	towel

Animals

l'abeille (f)	bee
l'animal (m)	animal
la bête	animal/creature
le cheval	horse
le cochon	pig
le coq	cockerel
l'oiseau (m)	bird
la poule	hen
le renard	fox
la souris	mouse
le taureau	bull
la vache	cow

The weather

le temps	the weather
l'averse (f)	shower (of rain)
le brouillard	fog
la brume	mist
la chaleur	heat
le ciel	sky
le climat	climate
le degré	degree
l'éclair (m)	flash of lightning
l'éclaircie (f)	bright period
la glace	ice
la météo	weather forecast
la neige	snow
le nuage	cloud
l'orage (m)	storm
la pluie	rain
la pression	pressure
le soleil	sun
la température	temperature
la tempête	storm
le tonnerre	thunder
le vent	wind
le verglas	black ice
la visibilité	visibility

Weather adjectives

agréable	pleasant
chaud(e)	hot
couvert(e)	cloudy/overcast
doux (douce)	mild
ensoleillé(e)	sunny
fort(e)	strong
frais (fraîche)	fresh/cool
froid(e)	cold
humide	damp
lourd(e)	heavy/sultry
orageux (orageuse)	stormy
pluvieux (pluvieuse)	rainy
sec (sèche)	dry
variable	variable

Weather verbs

briller	to shine
il fait beau/ chaud/froid	it is fine/hot/cold
il fait du vent	it is windy
il gèle/neige/ pleut	it is freezing/ snowing/raining
geler	to freeze
neiger	to snow
pleuvoir	to rain
tonner	to thunder

Tip These words are often tested in the listening and reading tests.

Colours, shapes & sizes

Colours

les couleurs *(f)*	colours	jaune	yellow
blanc (blanche)	white	marron	brown
bleu(e)	blue	noir(e)	black
blond(e)	blond	orange	orange
brun(e)	brown	pâle	pale
châtain	chestnut brown	rose	rose/pink
clair(e)	light/pale	rouge	red
la couleur	colour	roux (rousse)	reddish-brown/ ginger
de quelle couleur?	what colour?		
foncé(e)	dark	sombre	dark
gris(e)	grey	vert(e)	green
		violet (violette)	violet/purple

Adjectives combined with *clair* or *pâle* don't change when used with feminine or plural nouns.

Marron and orange don't change when used with feminine or plural nouns, and châtain doesn't add an *-e* in the feminine.

Shapes and sizes

aigu (aiguë)	sharp	haut(e)	tall/high
bas (basse)	low/small	large	wide
carré(e)	square	long (longue)	long
court(e)	short	petit(e)	small
énorme	enormous	plein(e)	full
épais (épaisse)	thick	rectangulaire	rectangular
étroit(e)	narrow	rond(e)	round
la forme	shape	la taille	size
grand(e)	big/tall	vide	empty
gros (grosse)	large/fat		

The world around us
Countries and nationalities

Countries & nationalities

French	English	French	English
le pays	country	la Grande-Bretagne	Great Britain
la capitale	capital	grec (grecque)	Greek
la nationalité	nationality	la Grèce	Greece
l'Allemagne (f)	Germany	hollandais(e)	Dutch
allemand(e)	German	la Hollande	Holland
américain(e)	American	irlandais(e)	Irish
anglais(e)	English	l'Irlande (du Nord) (f)	(Northern) Ireland
l'Angleterre (f)	England	l'Italie (f)	Italy
l'Autriche (f)	Austria	italien (-ienne)	Italian
autrichien (-enne)	Austrian	le Japon	Japan
belge	Belgian	japonais(e)	Japanese
la Belgique	Belgium	le Luxembourg	Luxembourg
britannique	British	luxembourgeois(e)	from Luxembourg
le Canada	Canada	le Maroc	Morocco
canadien (-ienne)	Canadian	marocain(e)	Maroccan
le Danemark	Denmark	le Pays de Galles	Wales
danois(e)	Danish	les Pays-Bas (m)	Netherlands
écossais(e)	Scottish	portugais(e)	Portuguese
l'Ecosse (f)	Scotland	le Portugal	Portugal
l'Espagne (f)	Spain	le Royaume-Uni	United Kingdom
espagnol(e)	Spanish	russe	Russian
les Etats-Unis (m)	USA	la Russie	Russia
l'Europe (f)	Europe	la Suède	Sweden
européen (-éenne)	European	suédois(e)	Swedish
finlandais(e)	Finnish	la Suisse	Switzerland
la Finlande	Finland	suisse	Swiss
français(e)	French		
la France	France		
gallois(e)	Welsh		

For more help see Success Guide page 27

VOCABULARY

58

Careers

At work

l'ambition (f)	ambition	les offres (f) d'emploi	job offers/ vacancies
l'annonce (f)	advertisement (job)	le patron/ la patronne	boss
bien payé(e)	well paid	la petite annonce	small ad
le boulot	job/work	le/la propriétaire	owner
le bureau	office	la publicité	advertising
la carrière	career	la réclame	advertisement (for goods)
la compagnie	company		
l'emploi (m)	job/post	la réunion	meeting
l'employé (m)/ l'employée (f)	employee	le salaire	salary
		seul(e)	alone/on your own
l'employeur (m)	employer	le stage	course
en équipe	in a team	le/la stagiaire	trainee
en plein air	in the open air	le tourisme	tourism
l'étudiant (m)/ l'étudiante (f)	student	le travail	work
		l'université (f)	university
expérimenté(e)	experienced	l'usine (f)	factory
la ferme	farm	la vie	life
la formation	training		
le gérant	manager		
l'interview (m)	interview		
la licence	(university) degree		
le magasin	shop		
mal payé(e)	badly paid		
le métier	job/career		

Tip You'll find these words useful if asked to describe your work experience in your coursework.

Verbs

adorer	to love	aimer bien	to like
s'adresser à	to apply to	aller	to go
aider	to help	s'approcher	to approach

continued on page 60

attacher	to attach	monter	to go up
appeler	to call	noter	to note
augmenter	to increase	obtenir	to obtain
avoir	to have	s'occuper de	to take care of
baisser	to lower	ouvrir	to open
bâtir	to build	paraître	to seem
collaborer	to work together	passer	to spend (time)
coller	to stick	se passer	to happen
conduire	to drive	penser	to think
continuer	to continue	porter	to carry
croire	to believe	poser (une question)	to put/to ask (a question)
découper	to cut out	pouvoir	to be able
déménager	to move house	promettre	to promise
demeurer	to stay/to remain	prononcer	to pronounce
descendre	to go down	quitter	to leave
diminuer	to reduce	raconter	to tell (a story)
diriger	to direct/manage	rappeler	to call back
distribuer	to distribute	refuser	to refuse
échouer (à un examen)	to fail (an exam)	regarder	to watch
employer	to employ/to use	répondre	to answer
enlever	to remove	respecter	to respect/observe (law etc.)
enregistrer	to record/to register/ to check in	rêver	to dream
enseigner	to teach	se souvenir de	to remember
entendre	to hear	surprendre	to surprise
être	to be	taper (à la machine)	to type
faire	to do	téléphoner	to phone
faire un stage	to go on a course	tirer	to pull
gérer	to run/manage	tomber	to fall
s'habituer à	to get used to	tomber malade	to fall ill
imaginer	to imagine	travailler	to work
inventer	to invent	vérifier	to check
laisser	to let/to leave		

Job titles

les affaires (f)	business	l'hôtesse de l'air (f)	air stewardess
l'agent de police (m)	policeman	l'infirmier (m)/ l'infirmière (f)	nurse
l'agriculteur (m)	farmer	l'informaticien (m)/ l'informaticienne (f)	computer operator
l'assistant(e)	PA	l'ingénieur (m)	engineer
l'avocat (m)	lawyer	l'instituteur (m)/ l'institutrice (f)	(primary school) teacher
le caissier/la caissière	cashier	le/la journaliste	journalist
le chauffeur	driver	le maire	mayor
le chauffeur de taxi	taxi driver	le marchand/ la marchande	trader/ shopkeeper
le/la chef	boss	le marin	sailor
le chirurgien/ la chirurgienne	surgeon	le mécanicien/ la mécanicienne	mechanic
le coiffeur/ la coiffeuse	hairdresser	le médecin	doctor
le commerçant/ la commerçante	trader/ shopkeeper	la ménagère	housewife
le/la comptable	accountant	l'opticien (m)/ l'opticienne (f)	optician
le/la concierge	caretaker	l'ouvrier (m)/ l'ouvrière (f)	worker
le contrôleur/ la contrôleuse	ticket inspector	le paysan/ la paysanne	peasant
le/la dentiste	dentist	le pilote	pilot/racing driver
le docteur	doctor	le plombier	plumber
le/la domestique	servant	le pompier	firefighter
le douanier/ la douanière	customs officer	le/la pompiste	pump attendant
l'écrivain (m)	writer	le routier	lorry driver
la femme d'affaires	businesswoman	le/la secrétaire	secretary
le fermier/ la fermière	farmer	le soldat	soldier
le gendarme	policeman	le technicien/ la technicienne	technician
l'homme d'affaires (m)	businessman	le vendeur/ la vendeuse	salesperson

Communications

On the telephone

l'annuaire *(m)*	*telephone book*
la cabine téléphonique	*telephone booth*
le coup de fil/ de téléphone	*phone call*
l'indicatif *(m)*	*code*
le répondeur automatique/ téléphonique	*answering machine*
la télécarte	*phone card*
le téléphone	*telephone*

On the Internet

la chatroom	*chatroom*
le courriel	*email (message)*
le courrier électronique	*email (messaging)*
l'email *(m)*	*email (message)*
l'Internet *(m)*	*the Internet*
parcourir le net	*to browse*
surfer sur le net	*to surf the net*

Telephone verbs

appeler	*to call*
attendre la tonalité	*to wait for the tone*
composer le numéro	*to dial the number*
décrocher (le téléphone)	*to pick up the phone*
écouter	*to listen*
entendre	*to hear*
envoyer un SMS	*to text*
laisser un message	*to leave a message*
rappeler	*to call back*
répondre	*to answer*
sonner	*to ring*
téléphoner	*to phone*
se tromper	*to make a mistake*
se tromper de numéro	*to get the wrong number*

Telephone expressions

allô	*hello (on the phone)*
à l'appareil	*speaking (on the phone)*
c'est de la part de qui?	*who is calling?*
ne quittez pas	*hold the line*

VOCABULARY

For more help see Success Guide pages **64** & **70**

Public transport

Means of transport

l'aéroglisseur (m)	hovercraft		la gare routière	bus station
l'aéroport (m)	airport		l'hovercraft (m)	hovercraft
l'arrêt (m)	stop		le kilomètre	kilometre
l'arrêt d'autobus (m)	bus stop		lent(e)	slow
s'arrêter	to stop		le métro	underground (train)
l'autobus (m)	bus		le numéro	number
l'autocar (m)	coach		à pied	on foot
l'avion (m)	plane		rapide	fast
le bateau	boat		la sortie	exit
le billet	ticket		la sortie de secours	emergency exit
le bus	bus		la station (de métro)	(underground) station
le camion	lorry			
le car	coach		le ticket	ticket (for travel)
le chemin de fer	railway		le train	train
la destination	destination		le tram(way)	tram
la distance	distance		les transports en commun (m)	public transport
en retard	late			
la gare	(railway) station		le tunnel	tunnel
la gare maritime	quayside station		le vol	flight

Une station is an underground station. *Une gare* is a mainline station.

Be careful with the word *car*: it means 'bus'! *Une voiture* is a car.

For more help see Success Guide page **31**

At the station

accès aux quais	*to the trains*		occupé(e)	*taken*
l'aller-retour *(m)*	*return ticket*		en provenance de	*coming from*
l'aller simple *(m)*	*single ticket*		le quai	*platform*
le billet simple	*single ticket*		la salle d'attente	*waiting room*
le compartiment	*compartment*		SNCF (la Société Nationale des Chemins de fer Français)	*French Railways*
composter	*to validate/ date-stamp (a ticket)*			
la consigne (automatique)	*left luggage (locker)*		le supplément	*supplement*
			le TGV (Train à Grande Vitesse)	*high-speed train*
la couchette	*couchette*		valable	*valid*
le départ	*departure*		la voie	*track*
à destination de	*going to*		le wagon-lit	*sleeping car*
direct(e)	*direct*		le wagon-restaurant	*dining car*
l'express *(m)*	*express train*		les W.-C. *(m)*	*toilets*
fumeur/ non-fumeur	*smoking/ non-smoking*			
le non-fumeur	*non-smoking compartment*			

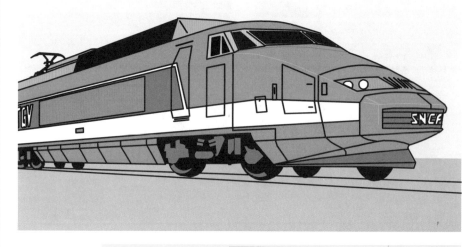

For more help see Success Guide pages **53** & **55**

On the road

l'auto (f)	car
l'autoroute (f)	motorway
la batterie	battery
la bicyclette	bicycle
la carte routière	road map
la ceinture de sécurité	seat belt
le coffre	boot (of car)
le conducteur	driver
dépanner	to repair (car)
la déviation	diversion
en panne	broken down
l'essence (f)	petrol
les essuie-glace (m)	windscreen wipers
le frein	brake
le/la garagiste	garage attendant
le gasoil/gazole	diesel
les heures d'affluence (f)	rush hour/peak period
l'huile (f)	oil
le litre	litre
la marque	make (of car etc.)
le moteur	engine
la moto(cyclette)	motorcycle
le numéro d'immatriculation	registration number
obligatoire	compulsory
le passage protégé	right of way
le péage	toll
le périphérique	ring road
le permis de conduire	driving licence
plein(e)	full
le pneu	tyre
le pneu crevé	puncture
le poids lourd	lorry
la portière	door (of vehicle)
la pression	(tyre) pressure
priorité à droite	give way to the right
le radiateur	radiator
réparer	to repair
la roue (de secours)	(spare) wheel
rouler	to travel/to drive
la route (nationale)	(main) road
sans plomb	unleaded
la station-service	filling station
le stationnement	parking
le super	high-grade petrol
le taxi	taxi
les travaux (m)	roadworks
le véhicule	vehicle
le vélo	bike
le vélomoteur	motorcycle
la vitesse	speed/gear
le volant	steering wheel
la voiture	car

For more help see Success Guide pages 44 & 75

Grammatical terms

Before you start your grammar revision, you need to familiarise yourself with some grammatical terms. You will find this section useful to refer back to.

Look at this sentence:

definite article   *adverb*   *indefinite article*   *noun (direct object)*   *definite article*

The girl quickly makes a delicious cake in the kitchen.

noun (subject)   *verb*   *adjective*   *preposition*   *noun*

- The **definite article** is the grammatical name given to the word **the**.
- The **indefinite article** is the name given to the word **a** or **an**.
- A **noun** is a person, place, thing or animal (e.g. Tom, London, chair, cat).
- A **verb** is a word that expresses an action (e.g. eats).
- An **adjective** is a word that describes a noun (e.g. delicious).
- An **adverb** is a word that describes a verb. It tells you how an action is done (e.g. quickly). Many adverbs in English end in **-ly**.
- A **preposition** is a word placed before a noun or a pronoun to indicate time, place or condition (e.g. **in** the kitchen).
- A **conjunction** is a word that links two parts of a sentence (e.g. He was eating **and** drinking.) The most common conjunctions in English are 'and' and 'but'.
- A **pronoun** is a word that stands in place of a noun. In the sentence above, we could replace the noun 'the girl' with the pronoun 'she'. Similarly, 'a cake' could be replaced by 'it'.
- A **relative pronoun** is a word that links one part of a sentence to a person or thing in another part of the sentence. In English the relative pronons are 'who', 'whom', 'which', 'that' (e.g. in 'I gave him all the money **that** I earned', 'I gave him all the money' and 'I earned' are linked by the relative pronoun 'that', which refers back to 'money').
- A **negative** is a word that indicates that an action is not being done (e.g. not, never).
- **Gender** refers to whether a word is masculine or feminine.
- The **subject** is the name given to the person or thing doing the action. In the sentence above, the subject is 'the girl'.
- The **direct object** is the name given to the person or thing that has the action done directly to it. In the sentence above, 'a cake' is the object because it is made by the girl.

Articles

The indefinite article

This is the grammatical way of referring to 'a' or 'an'.

- Use **un** before a masculine noun.
- Use **une** before a feminine noun.

To a ... is **à un** ... or **à une** ...

à un match	to a match
à une école	to a school

Of a ... is **d'un** ... or **d'une** ...

le toit **d'un** château	the roof **of a** castle
le toit **d'une** maison	the roof **of a** house

Tip Leave out *un* and *une* when stating a person's job: *Il est professeur* 'He is a teacher'.

The definite article

This is the grammatical way of referring to 'the'.

- Use **le** before a masculine singular noun. **Le** is shortened to **l'** before a word that starts with a vowel or **h**.

le chien	the dog	l'homme	the man

- Use **la** before a feminine singular noun. **La** is shortened to **l'** before a word that starts with a vowel or **h**.

la table	the table	l'église	the church

- Use **les** before all plural nouns.

les tables	the tables	les hommes	the men

There are four ways of saying 'to the':

1 **au** before masculine singular nouns

Je vais **au** cinéma.	I am going to the cinema.

2 **à la** before feminine singular nouns

Je vais **à la** mairie.	I am going to the town hall.

3 **à l'** before singular nouns beginning with a vowel or **h**

Je vais **à l'**université.	I am going to the university.

4 **aux** before all plural nouns

Je vais **aux** Etats-Unis.	I am going to the USA.

There are four ways of saying 'of the':

1 **du** before masculine singular nouns
   la fille **du** professeur   *the teacher's daughter*

2 **de la** before feminine singular nouns
   le fils **de la** secrétaire   *the secretary's daughter*

3 **de l'** before singular nouns beginning with a vowel or **h**
   le chapeau **de l'**homme   *the man's hat*

4 **des** before all plural nouns
   les parents **des** jeunes   *the young people's parents*

The partitive article

This is the grammatical way of referring to 'some/any'.

- **Du** is used before masculine singular nouns.
- **De la** is used before feminine singular nouns.
- **De l'** is used before singular nouns beginning with a vowel.
- **Des** is used before all plural nouns.

Aujourd'hui je vais au supermarché. Je vais acheter **du** pain, **de la** crème, **de l'**eau et **des** fraises.

Today I am going to the supermarket. I am going to buy some bread, some cream, some water and some strawberries.

Nouns and adjectives

Gender of nouns

Tip When you learn nouns, it's vital to learn their gender too. Don't just learn *stylo* = 'pen', learn *un stylo* = 'a pen' so that you remember that *stylo* is masculine.

In French, every noun, whether it refers to something living or not, is either masculine or feminine. For example:

masculine		feminine	
un stylo	*a pen*	une montre	*a watch*
un taureau	*a bull*	une femme	*a woman*

usually masculine	usually feminine
male people and animals	female people and animals
days, months and seasons	nouns ending in *-ette*
weights and measures	nouns ending in *-ie* (e.g. many shops)
languages	nouns ending in *-ille*
trees	nouns ending in *-sion* and *-tion*
points of the compass	nouns ending in *-té*
nouns ending in *-age*	nouns ending in *-ure*
nouns ending in *-eau*	
nouns ending in *-ier*	
nouns ending in *-ment*	
nouns ending in *-oir*	

The gender of some nouns depends on whether the person is male or female.

un élève	*a pupil (boy)*	une élève	*a pupil (girl)*
un touriste	*a tourist (male)*	une touriste	*a tourist (female)*

Other nouns don't change their gender, whether they are referring to a male or a female.

un professeur	*a teacher (male or female)*
un médecin	*a doctor (male or female)*
une victime	*a victim (male or female)*
une personne	*a person (male or female)*

Plural of nouns

As in English, to make a noun plural you usually add **-s**.

| la chaise | *chair* | les chaises | *chairs* |
| le chien | *dog* | les chiens | *dogs* |

Words that end in **-al** change to **-aux** in the plural.

le cheval	*the horse*	les chevaux	*the horses*
l'animal	*the animal*	les animaux	*the animals*
le journal	*the newspaper*	les journaux	*the newspapers*

Words that end in **-eau** add **-x** in the plural.

le cadeau	*the present*	les cadeaux	*the presents*
le château	*the castle*	les châteaux	*the castles*
l'oiseau	*the bird*	les oiseaux	*the birds*

These common nouns have irregular plurals:

le bijou	*the jewel*	les bijoux	*the jewels*
le fils	*son*	les fils	*sons*
le jeu	*the game*	les jeux	*the games*
l'œil	*the eye*	les yeux	*the eyes*

Tip *These plurals have to be learnt individually.*

Agreement of adjectives

Adjectives change their endings to 'agree' with the noun they are used with. In dictionaries and wordlists, they are listed in the form used with masculine singular nouns.

Most adjectives change as follows:

- If an adjective describes a feminine singular noun, add **-e**.
- If an adjective describes a masculine plural noun, add **-s**.
- If an adjective describes a feminine plural noun, add **-es**.

un crayon bleu	*a blue pencil*
une voiture bleu**e**	*a blue car*
deux crayons bleu**s**	*two blue pencils*
deux voitures bleu**es**	*two blue cars*

- If the adjective already ends in **-e**, do not add another **-e** in the feminine.

| un crayon rouge | *a red pencil* |
| une voiture rouge | *a red car* |

deux crayons rouge**s**	*two red pencils*
deux voitures rouge**s**	*two red cars*

- If an adjective already ends in **-s**, do not add another **-s** in the plural.

un crayon gris	*a grey pencil*
une voiture gris**e**	*a grey car*
deux crayons gris	*two grey pencils*
deux voitures gris**es**	*two grey cars*

- Adjectives that end in **-eux** or **-oux** change to **-euse** or **-ouse** in the feminine.

un garçon heureux	*a happy boy*
une fille heureu**se**	*a happy girl*
deux hommes jaloux	*two jealous men*
deux femmes jalou**ses**	*two jealous women*

- Adjectives that end in **-eau**, **-er**, **-f**, **-ien**, **-il** change as follows in the feminine:

un beau garçon	*a beautiful boy*
une belle fille	*a beautiful girl*
le premier homme	*the first man*
la première femme	*the first woman*
un homme sportif	*an athletic man*
une femme sportive	*an athletic woman*
un vélo neuf	*a brand new bike*
une voiture neuve	*a brand new car*
un homme italien	*an Italian man*
une femme italienne	*an Italian woman*
un gentil homme	*a nice man*
une gentille femme	*a nice woman*

- These common adjectives have irregular feminine forms:

masculine	feminine	
blanc	blanche	*white*
bon	bonne	*good*
cher	chère	*dear*
favori	favorite	*favourite*
frais	fraîche	*fresh*
gros	grosse	*big*
long	longue	*long*
secret	secrète	*secret*
vieux	vieille	*old*

Tip

These feminine forms have to be learnt individually.

Position of adjectives

Most adjectives come **after** the noun, e.g. *un livre rouge* (not *un rouge livre*).

These common adjectives usually come **before** the noun:

beau	*beautiful*	long	*long*
bon	*good*	mauvais	*bad*
gentil	*nice*	nouveau	*new*
grand	*big*	petit	*small*
jeune	*young*	vieux	*old*
joli	*pretty*		

The position of an adjective can change its meaning, e.g. *un cher ami* is a dear friend, but *un livre cher* is an expensive book.

Demonstrative adjectives

The demonstrative adjectives in English are 'this', 'that', 'these', 'those'. In French they are as follows:

ce journal	*this paper, that paper*	(masculine singular)
cet ami	*this friend, that friend*	(masculine singular beginning with a vowel)
cette table	*this table, that table*	(feminine singular)
ces élèves	*these pupils, those pupils*	(plural)

Possessive adjectives

The possessive adjectives ('my', 'your', etc.) describe who something belongs to.

	masc. sing.	fem. sing.	plural
my	**mon** livre	**ma** chaise	**mes** livres
your (singular)	**ton** livre	**ta** chaise	**tes** livres
his/her	**son** livre	**sa** chaise	**ses** livres
our	**notre** père	**notre** famille	**nos** familles
your (plural/polite sing.)	**votre** père	**votre** famille	**vos** familles
their	**leur** père	**leur** famille	**leurs** familles

For ease of pronunciation, *mon*, *ton* and *son* are also used before feminine nouns beginning with a vowel or *h*, e.g. *mon amie*.

French possessive adjectives agree in gender with the person or thing owned, not with the owner: *sa sœur* 'his/her sister', *son père* 'his/her father'.

Tip

Pronouns

Subject pronouns

Je becomes *j'* before a vowel: *j'aime* 'I like', *j'adore* 'I love'.

A subject pronoun is used for the subject of the verb: it refers to the person who does the action.

Note that there are two ways of saying 'you':

Je parle.	*I speak.*	**Nous** parlons.	*We speak.*
Tu parles.	*You speak.*	**Vous** parlez.	*You speak.*
Il parle.	*He speaks.*	**Ils** parlent.	*They speak.*
Elle parle.	*She speaks.*	**Elles** parlent.	*They speak.*

- Use *tu* (familiar 'you') when talking to a member of your family or a close friend.
- Use *vous* (formal 'you') when talking to someone you don't know well.
- When talking to more than one person, always use *vous*.

There are also two ways of saying 'they':
- Use *ils* when 'they' refers to a masculine group.
- Use *elles* when 'they' refers to a feminine group.
- If the group is mixed i.e. both masculine and feminine, use *ils*.

Direct object pronouns

Me, te, le and *la* become *m', t', l'* before a vowel: *il m'aime* 'he loves me'.

A direct object pronoun is used for the object of the verb: it refers to the person or thing that has the action done to it.

Il **me** voit.	*He sees me.*	Il **nous** voit.	*He sees us.*
Il **te** voit.	*He sees you.*	Il **vous** voit.	*He sees you.*
Il **le** voit.	*He sees him.*	Il **les** voit.	*He sees them.*
Il **la** voit.	*He sees her.*		

Indirect object pronouns

Me and *te* become *m'* and *t'* before a vowel: *il t'a donné le cadeau* 'he gave the present to you'.

The indirect object pronoun refers to the person or thing that receives the direct object. In English it is usually preceded by 'to', but sometimes the 'to' is hidden.

He gave the present **to me**.   *or*   He gave me the present.
He sent the letter **to him**.   *or*   He sent him the present.

me	*to me*	nous	*to us*
te	*to you (familiar)*	vous	*to you (formal or plural)*
lui	*to him/to her/to it*	leur	*to them (masculine or feminine)*

Negatives

In French, negatives usually consist of two words, which 'sandwich' the verb.

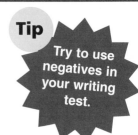

ne … pas	*not*
ne … jamais	*never*
ne … personne	*nobody/no one*
ne … ni … (ni …)	*neither … nor …*
ne … plus	*not any more, no longer*
ne … rien	*nothing*

Il **n'**est **pas** venu.	*He did not come.*
Il **ne** paie **jamais**.	*He never pays.*
Je **ne** vois **personne**.	*I see nobody.*
Elle **n'**est **ni** riche **ni** pauvre.	*She is neither rich nor poor.*
Je **n'**habite **plus** à Londres.	*I don't live in London any more.*
Elle **ne** mange **rien**.	*She eats nothing.*

Le jour de mon anniversaire, je **n'**ai **pas** reçu l'argent que mes parents m'avaient promis.

On my birthday I didn't get the money that my parents had promised me.

J'aime le tennis mais je **ne** joue **jamais** au football.

I like tennis but I never play football.

GRAMMAR

Verbs

The present tense

You use the present tense to say what is happening now and what usually happens.

The infinitive minus its -er/-ir/-re ending is the 'stem' of the verb.

REGULAR -ER VERBS

Remove the **-er** ending from the infinitive and add these endings:

regarder – to look	
je regard**e**	I look
tu regard**es**	you (singular) look
il/elle regard**e**	he/she looks
nous regard**ons**	we look
vous regard**ez**	you (plural/polite singular) look
ils/elles regard**ent**	they look

The endings are: -e, -es, -e, -ons, -ez, -ent

Other verbs like **regarder** (i.e. regular **-er** verbs):

arriver	to arrive
chanter	to sing
chercher	to look for
commencer	to begin (nous commençons – we begin)
donner	to give
habiter	to live
manger	to eat (nous mangeons – we eat)
marcher	to walk
préparer	to prepare
trouver	to find

In the nous form, to keep the pronunciation the same, c changes to ç and an e is added after g.

REGULAR -*IR* VERBS

Remove the -*ir* ending from the infinitive and add these endings:

finir – *to finish*	
je finis	nous finissons
tu finis	vous finissez
il/elle finit	ils/elles finissent

The endings are: -*is*, -*is*, -*it*, -*issons*, *issez*, -*issent*

Other verbs like *finir* (i.e. regular -*ir* verbs):

bâtir	*to build*	remplir	*to fill*
choisir	*to choose*		

REGULAR -*RE* VERBS

Remove the -*re* ending from the infinitive and add these endings:

vendre – *to sell*	
je vends	nous vendons
tu vends	vous vendez
il/elle vend	ils/elles vendent

The endings are: -*s*, -*s*, -, -*ons*, -*ez*, -*ent*

Other verbs like *vendre* (i.e. regular -*ir* verbs):

attendre	*to wait for*	perdre	*to lose*
descendre	*to go down*	rendre	*to give back*
entendre	*to hear*	répondre	*to answer*

IRREGULAR PRESENT-TENSE VERBS

Unfortunately, some of the commonest French verbs do not follow the above rules: they are irregular. You have to learn them individually. Here are the essential ones.

aller – *to go*	
je vais	nous allons
tu vas	vous allez
il/elle va	ils/elles vont

avoir – *to have*	
j'ai	nous avons
tu as	vous avez
il/elle a	ils/elles ont

boire – *to drink*	
je bois	nous buvons
tu bois	vous buvez
il/elle boit	ils/elles boivent

connaître – *to know (a person or a place)*	
je connais	nous connaissons
tu connais	vous connaissez
il/elle connaît	ils/elles connaissent

courir – *to run*	
je cours	nous courons
tu cours	vous courez
il/elle court	ils/elles courent

croire – to believe	
je crois	nous croyons
tu crois	vous croyez
il/elle croit	ils/elles croient

devoir – to have to, must	
je dois	nous devons
tu dois	vous devez
il/elle doit	ils/elles doivent

dire – to say, to tell	
je dis	nous disons
tu dis	vous dites
il/elle dit	ils/elles disent

dormir – to sleep	
je dors	nous dormons
tu dors	vous dormez
il/elle dort	ils/elles dorment

écrire – to write	
j'écris	nous écrivons
tu écris	vous écrivez
il/elle écrit	ils/elles écrivent

être – to be	
je suis	nous sommes
tu es	vous êtes
il/elle est	ils/elles sont

faire – to do, to make	
je fais	nous faisons
tu fais	vous faites
il/elle fait	ils/elles font

lire – to read	
je lis	nous lisons
tu lis	vous lisez
il/elle lit	ils/elles lisent

mettre – to put	
je mets	nous mettons
tu mets	vous mettez
il/elle met	ils/elles mettent

partir – to leave	
je pars	nous partons
tu pars	vous partez
il/elle part	ils/elles partent

pouvoir – to be able to, can	
je peux	nous pouvons
tu peux	vous pouvez
il/elle peut	ils/elles peuvent

prendre – to take	
je prends	nous prenons
tu prends	vous prenez
il/elle prend	ils/elles prennent

recevoir – to receive	
je reçois	nous recevons
tu reçois	vous recevez
il/elle reçoit	ils/elles reçoivent

rire – to laugh	
je ris	nous rions
tu ris	vous riez
il/elle rit	ils/elles rient

savoir – to know (a fact)	
je sais	nous savons
tu sais	vous savez
il/elle sait	ils/elles savent

venir – to come	
je viens	nous venons
tu viens	vous venez
il/elle vient	ils/elles viennent

voir – to see	
je vois	nous voyons
tu vois	vous voyez
il/elle voit	ils/elles voient

vouloir – to wish, to want	
je veux	nous voulons
tu veux	vous voulez
il/elle veut	ils/elles veulent

The perfect tense

The perfect tense is used to say what has happened, what happened or what did happen in the past.

> Il a joué au football.
> *He has played football/He played football/ He did play football.*

To form the perfect tense you need the present tense of either **avoir** or **être** and a past participle.

Tip

You use the perfect when the action has been finished – 'perfected'. If it hasn't been finished, use the *depuis* construction (see page 87).

THE PAST PARTICIPLE

To find a past participle in English, put 'I have' in front of the verb. For example, the past participle of 'to write' is 'written' and the past participle of 'to go' in English is 'gone'.

To form the past participle of French verbs:

* **-er** verbs: remove the **-er** and add **-é**
  donner → donn → **donné**
* **-ir** verbs: remove the **-ir** and add **-i**
  finir → fin → **fini**
* **-re** verbs: remove the **-re** and add **-u**
  vendre → vend → **vendu**

VERBS THAT TAKE *AVOIR*

The vast majority of French verbs use **avoir** for the perfect tense. Examples:

donner	finir
j'ai donné *(I gave, I have given)*	j'ai fini *(I finished, I have finished)*
tu as donné	tu as fini
il/elle a donné	il/elle a fini
nous avons donné	nous avons fini
vous avez donné	vous avez fini
ils/elles ont donné	ils/elles ont fini

vendre
j'ai vendu *(I sold, I have sold)*
tu as vendu
il/elle a vendu
nous avons vendu
vous avez vendu
ils/elles ont vendu

These common *avoir* verbs have irregular past participles:

infinitive	perfect tense	
avoir	j'ai eu	*I had, I have had*
boire	j'ai bu	*I drank, I have drunk*
connaître	j'ai connu	*I knew, I have known*
courir	j'ai couru	*I ran, I have run*
croire	j'ai cru	*I believed, I have believed*
devoir	j'ai dû	*I had to/I owed, I have had to/owed*
dire	j'ai dit	*I said, I have said*
écrire	j'ai écrit	*I wrote, I have written*
être	j'ai été	*I was, I have been*
faire	j'ai fait	*I made/did, I have made/done*
lire	j'ai lu	*I read, I have read*
mettre	j'ai mis	*I put, I have put*
ouvrir	j'ai ouvert	*I opened, I have opened*
pleuvoir	il a plu	*it rained, it has rained*
pouvoir	j'ai pu	*I have been able to, I was able to*
prendre	j'ai pris	*I took, I have taken*
recevoir	j'ai reçu	*I received, I have received*
rire	j'ai ri	*I laughed, I have laughed*
savoir	j'ai su	*I knew, I have known*
suivre	j'ai suivi	*I followed, I have followed*
vivre	j'ai vécu	*I lived, I have lived*
voir	j'ai vu	*I saw, I have seen*
vouloir	j'ai voulu	*I wanted, I have wanted*

VERBS THAT TAKE *ÊTRE*

These verbs form the perfect tense with *être*:

With these verbs, the past participle has to agree with the subject. This means that you have to add **-e**, **-s** or **-es** to the past participle if the subject is feminine singular, masculine plural or feminine plural.

Tip

All of these are 'verbs of motion', apart from *mourir* and *naître*, *devenir* and *rester*.

Tip

A group of men and women together is treated as masculine!

aller	to go
arriver	to arrive
descendre	to go down
devenir	to become
entrer	to enter
monter	to go up
mourir	to die
naître	to be born
partir	to leave
rentrer	to go back
rester	to stay
retourner	to return
revenir	to come back
sortir	to go out
tomber	to fall
venir	to come

If a man wanted to say 'I arrived yesterday', he would say **Je suis arrivé hier**. But a woman would say **Je suis arrivée hier**. If two men wanted to say 'We arrived yesterday', they would say **Nous sommes arrivés hier**. But a group of women would say **Nous sommes arrivées hier**.

These **être** verbs have irregular past participles:

infinitive	perfect tense	
mourir	il est mort/elle est morte	*he/she died, he/she has died*
naître	je suis né(e)	*I was born*
venir*	nous sommes venu(e)s	*we came, we have come*

* Also **revenir – revenu(e)** and **devenir – devenu(e)**

REFLEXIVE VERBS

Reflexive verbs also form the perfect tense with **être**. Example:

se laver
je me suis lavé(e) *(I washed (myself))*
tu t'es lavé(e)
il s'est lavé/elle s'est lavée

nous nous sommes lavé(e)s
vous vous êtes lavé(e)(s)
ils se sont lavés/elles se sont lavées

The imperfect tense

This tense is so called because it is used for an action that has not been 'perfected' or finished. It says what used to happen or what was happening at some point in the past. Its three main uses are:

1 To say what someone was doing or what was happening.

Je **lisais** un livre quand tu es entré.
I was reading a book when you came in.
Elle **regardait** la télé quand le téléphone a sonné.
She was watching the TV when the phone rang.
Ils **écoutaient** la radio toute la soirée.
They were listening to the radio all evening.

Note that the first two examples have an imperfect tense followed by a perfect tense: something was going on when something else interrupted it. What was going on is in the imperfect tense and what interrupted it is in the perfect tense.

2 To say what habitually used to happen.

J'**allais** le voir le mercredi.   *I used to go and see him on Wednesdays.*
Il **mangeait** trop.   *He used to eat too much.*

3 To describe a situation in the past.

Il **faisait** froid.   *It was cold.*
Elle ne **voulait** pas sortir avec moi.   *She did not want to go out with me.*

To find the imperfect tense stem, take the ***nous*** form of the present tense and remove the **-ons**, e.g.

Tip The endings for all verbs are: -ais, -ais, -ait, -ions, -iez, -aient

finir *(to finish)* → nous finissons *(we finish)* → **finiss-**

Then add these endings to the stem:

donner	finir	vendre
je donnais *(I was giving)*	je finissais *(I was finishing)*	je vendais *(I was selling)*
tu donnais	tu finissais	tu vendais
il/elle donnait	il/elle finissait	il/elle vendait
nous donnions	nous finissions	nous vendions
vous donniez	vous finissiez	vous vendiez
ils/elles donnaient	ils/elles finissaient	ils/elles vendaient

Être has the only irregular stem:

être	
j'étais *(I was)*	nous étions
tu étais	vous étiez
il/elle était	ils/elles étaient

Tip To pick up some marks in tests, learn two or three imperfect forms by heart and include them, e.g. *Il pleuvait* 'It was raining', *Je portais mon pull neuf* 'I was wearing my new pullover'.

The future tense

The future tense is used to say what will happen or what someone will do in the future. In English we can use 'will' or 'shall', both often abbreviated to ''ll'.

j'**irai**	*I will go/I shall go/I'll go*
je n'**irai** pas	*I will not go/I shall not go/*
	I won't go/
	I shan't go

The endings for all verbs are: -ai, -as, -a, -ons, -ez, -ont

REGULAR -*ER* VERBS

The future endings are added to the whole of the infinitive.

Tip These are the same as the endings of the present tense of *avoir*.

donner	
je donnerai *(I shall give)*	nous donnerons
tu donneras	vous donnerez
il/elle donnera	ils/elles donneront

REGULAR -*IR* VERBS

The future endings are added to the whole of the infinitive.

finir	
je finirai *(I shall finish)*	nous finirons
tu finiras	vous finirez
il/elle finira	ils/elles finiront

REGULAR -*RE* VERBS

Remove the final **-e** of the infinitive before adding the endings.

vendre	
je vendrai *(I shall sell)*	nous vendrons
tu vendras	vous vendrez
il/elle vendra	ils/elles vendront

IRREGULAR FUTURE-TENSE VERBS

These common verbs have irregular future stems, but their endings are regular:

infinitive	perfect tense	
aller	j'irai	*I shall go*
avoir	j'aurai	*I shall have*
devoir	je devrai	*I shall have to*
envoyer	j'enverrai	*I shall send*
être	je serai	*I shall be*
faire	je ferai	*I shall do/make*
pouvoir	je pourrai	*I shall be able to*
recevoir	je recevrai	*I shall receive*
savoir	je saurai	*I shall know*
venir	je viendrai	*I shall come*
voir	je verrai	*I shall see*
vouloir	je voudrai	*I shall want*

Tip

The future stem always ends in *-r*, whether the verb is regular or irregular.

OTHER WAYS OF TALKING ABOUT THE FUTURE

In both French and English, instead of saying what you 'will do' in the future, you can say what you 'are going to do' or what you 'are doing' in the future.

Demain je jouerai au football.	*Tomorrow I will play football.*
= Demain je **vais jouer** au football.	= *Tomorrow I am going to play football.*
= Demain je **joue** au football.	= *Tomorrow I am playing football.*

The conditional

The conditional is used to say what would happen or what someone would do under certain conditions. You can recognise the conditional in English by the word 'would', often abbreviated to ''d'.

> Si j'étais riche, je voyagerais autour du monde.
> *If I were rich, I would travel round the world.*
> Si nous avions le temps, nous visiterions le musée.
> *If we had time, we would visit the museum.*
> Je voudrais aller en France en été.
> *I would like to go to France in summer.*

Notice how, in the first two examples, the first verb (the one following *si*, 'if') is in the imperfect tense and the second verb is in the conditional.

The endings for all verbs are:
-ais, -ais, -ait,
-ions, -iez, -aient

Tip

These are the same as the imperfect tense endings, but in the conditional they are added to the infinitive.

REGULAR -ER VERBS

The conditional endings are added to the whole of the infinitive.

donner	
je donnerais *(I would give)*	nous donnerions
tu donnerais	vous donneriez
il/elle donnerait	ils/elles donneraient

REGULAR -IR VERBS

The conditional endings are added to the whole of the infinitive.

finir	
je finirais *(I would finish)*	nous finirions
tu finirais	vous finiriez
il/elle finirait	ils/elles finiraient

REGULAR -*RE* VERBS

Drop the final **-e** of the infinitive before adding the endings.

vendre

je vendrais *(I would sell)*	nous vendrions
tu vendrais	vous vendriez
il/elle vendrait	ils/elles vendraient

IRREGULAR CONDITIONALS

The verbs that have irregular stems in the future tense use the same stems for the conditional. Their endings are regular.

infinitive	conditional	
aller	j'irais	*I would go*
avoir	j'aurais	*I would have*
devoir	je devrais	*I would have to*
envoyer	j'enverrais	*I would send*
être	je serais	*I would be*
faisre	je ferais	*I would do/make*
pouvoir	je pourrais	*I would be able to*
recevoir	je recevrais	*I would receive*
savoir	je saurais	*I would know*
venir	je viendrais	*I would come*
voir	je verrais	*I would see*
vouloir	je voudrais	*I would want*

Tip You will get extra marks for using a conditional. The easiest one to use is *Je voudrais*, 'I would like', e.g. *Je voudrais aller à l'université*.

The pluperfect tense

The pluperfect tense is used to say what had happened. It goes further back into the past than the perfect tense. The word 'pluperfect' means 'more than perfect': the action has not only been 'perfected' or completed, but something else has happened since.

> Quand je suis arrivé, les enfants **avaient** déjà **bu** toute la limonade.
> *When I arrived, the children had already finished off all the lemonade.*
> Elle **était** déjà **partie** quand j'ai téléphoné.
> *She had already left when I phoned.*
> Il était en retard parce qu'il **avait perdu** l'adresse.
> *He was late because he had lost the address.*
> J'**avais** déjà **vu** le film.
> *I had seen the film already.*

The pluperfect tense is also used to report what someone said.

> Direct speech: 'J'ai vu l'accident.'   *'I saw the accident.'*
> Reported speech: J'ai dit que j'**avais vu** l'accident. *I said that I had seen the accident.*

To form the pluperfect tense you need the imperfect tense of either *avoir* or *être* and a past participle.

PLUPERFECT TENSE WITH *AVOIR*

donner

j'avais donné *(I had given)*	nous avions donné
tu avais donné	vous aviez donné
il/elle avait donné	ils/elles avaient donné

PLUPERFECT TENSE WITH *ÊTRE*

aller

j'étais allé(e) *(I had gone)*	nous étions allé(e)s
tu étais allé(e)	vous étiez allé(e)(s)
il/elle était allé(e)	ils/elles étaient allé(e)s

Tip

The verbs that take *être* in the perfect tense also take *être* in the pluperfect.

Tip

You will get extra marks for using a pluperfect in your written work. Why not learn a few examples and include them?

Venir de ...

The French don't say 'I have just done something', they say 'I come from doing something'. They build it like this:

1 present tense of **venir**

2 **de**

3 infinitive of the verb describing the action.

> Je viens d'arriver. *I have just arrived.*

> For the present tense of *venir*, see page 77.

Depuis

Use **depuis** (since) to say how long you have been doing something that you are still doing.

> J'habite Londres depuis deux ans.
> *I have been living in London for two years.*

The French don't say 'I have been living in London for two years', they say 'I live in London since two years'. They build it like this:

1 present tense (even though the English uses the perfect tense)

2 **depuis**

3 time expression.

> Je regarde la télé depuis vingt minutes.
> *I have been watching TV for 20 minutes.*
> J'étudie le français depuis cinq ans.
> *I have been studying French for five years.*

Writing Coursework

What you need to know about Writing Coursework

- For GCSE French you have to do either a writing exam or Writing Coursework.
- Ask your teacher if you are being entered for the terminal exam or the coursework option.
- If you are doing coursework you have to submit three pieces of work.
- To get a top grade, each piece of work will need to be about 150–200 words long.
- With some exam boards you can choose your own title. Other boards give you a list of titles to choose from. Check with your teacher.

What makes a good piece of coursework

This is what the examiners are looking for:

- variety of tenses
- complex constructions
- longer sentences
- opinions
- justification of opinions
- impressive vocabulary
- well organised, imaginative and interesting reading

How to get started

You have to write a piece of coursework. Follow these **five** steps.

FIRST STEP

Choose a title. (You must talk to your teacher. You may be able to choose your own or you may have one chosen for you!)
Here are some ideas.

a) leaflet about my local area
b) letter of complaint to a holiday company (or a hotel or the Prime Minister!)
c) job application letter
d) my work experience
e) a famous person
f) an accident or incident
g) my favourite leisure activity
h) a trip abroad
i) review of a film, book, TV programme or play
j) "I've won ...!" (This title allows you to use your imagination.)
k) letter to a problem page

SECOND STEP

Make a list in English of things you can say about your topic.
If you are going for 150–170 words you will probably need at least 15 items on your list.

THIRD STEP

Rearrange your list into a logical sequence.

FOURTH STEP

Find out how to say the things on your list in French. You can use any book or reference material. Ask your teacher for suggestions.

FIFTH STEP

To get an A* in your coursework you must use as many of these structures as you can.

- present
- perfect with avoir, être + reflexive + irregular past participle
- future
- conditional
- pluperfect
- imperfect
- unusual vocabulary
- longer sequences – multiple use of parce que, car, puisque, donc
- opinions + justifications
- avoir constructions e.g. avoir peur, avoir besoin de, avoir envie de, avoir l'air ..., avoir lieu, avoir sommeil, en avoir marre.
- unusual weather constructions: il pleuvait à verse
- si beau, malgré, un tel accident
- exclamations e.g Quel cauchemar!
- before, after, on doing something
- venir de, sur le point de
- comparatives, superlatives.
- Preceding Direct Object
- direct/indirect object pronouns
- change of time sequence
- time phrases e.g. puis, ensuite
- Negatives – personne, jamais etc
- Subjunctive(s)
- Il y a trois ans,
- il y a trois ans que ...
- depuis
- A proverb? Tout est bien qui finit bien

Example of a coursework task

Write a description of your work experience.
(Target: 150–200 words)

What you could say

- Say who organised the work experience, when you did it and for how long.
- Say how you got there every morning and how you returned home.
- Say whether or not you liked the journey. Give a reason (tiring, expensive, long?).
- Say where you were working (in an office, out of doors, in a factory?).
- Say what you had to do at work (answer the phone, help someone, write letters, make tea, help in the office, look after children, look after sick people?).
- Say whether or not you liked the work and give reasons.
- Say whether or not you were paid.
- Say what you will do with the money.
- Describe a person that you worked with (the boss?).
- Say what you had for lunch and where you ate.
- Say what you did in the evenings after work.
- Say how you felt when you returned to school.
- Say whether or not you would like to do a similar job in the future. Give reasons.
- Say what your brother/sister/friend will do on his/her work experience. Give an opinion.

There are more than enough ideas here. You would select your own.

Writing your ideas in French

This is the hard bit! Use these word lists and any books or websites you can find to make your work attractive to the examiner.

Time expressions

au mois de février	*in February*
il y a deux mois	*two months ago*
le matin	*in the mornings*
le soir	*in the evenings*
tous les jours	*every day*
toute la journée	*all day*
d'abord	*first of all*
de temps en temps	*from time to time*
après, ensuite	*after, next*
en arrivant	*when I arrived*
en rentrant chez moi	*when I got home*
pendant une semaine	*for a week*
à l'avenir	*in the future*

The places

le bureau	*office*
en plein air	*out of doors*
le magasin	*shop*
l'usine *(f)*	*factory*
la cantine	*dining area/ canteen*

The people

le patron/ la patronne	*boss*
les ouvriers *(m)*/ les ouvrières *(f)*	*workers*
le/la secrétaire	*secretary*
le client/la cliente	*customer*
les collègues *(m/f)*	*workmates*
le professeur	*teacher*
les enfants *(m/f)*	*children*
les malades *(m/f)*	*sick people*

92

Useful words

fatigant(e)	*tiring*
cher (chère)	*expensive*
long (longue)	*long*
le stage	*work experience*
un tel travail	*a similar job*
parce que	*because*
quel travail!	*what a job!*
ennuyeux (-euse)	*boring*
ça m'a vraiment plu	*I really liked it*
trop	*too*
gentil (gentille)/sympa	*nice*
bruyant(e)	*noisy*

Verbs

j'aimais	*I liked/I used to like*
je n'aimais pas	*I didn't like*
j'adorais	*I loved*
je détestais	*I hated*
j'étais	*I was (e.g. tired)*
il/elle était	*he/she was*
je mangeais	*I ate/I used to eat*
je buvais	*I drank/I used to drink*
je dormais	*I slept/I used to sleep*
je travaillais	*I was working*
je devais …	*I had to …*
répondre au téléphone	*to answer the phone*
aider	*to help*

écrire des lettres	*to write letters*
faire le thé	*to make the tea*
organiser	*to organise*
voyager	*to travel*
rentrer à la maison	*to return home*
soigner	*to look after*
j'ai fait	*I did/I made*
j'ai reçu … livres	*I got … pounds*
je n'ai pas reçu …	*I did not get …*
j'irai	*I will go*
j'achèterai	*I will buy*

Sample piece of coursework

1 mark-winning time phrases

2 correct use of perfect tense

3 correct use of pluperfect tense

Mon Stage

Il y a deux mois, (1) au mois de février, j'ai (2) fait un stage dans un hôtel près de chez moi. Un de mes professeurs avait (3) organisé le stage qui a (2) duré une semaine. Tous les (1) jours, je (4) prenais le car à six heures du matin. Je (4) rentrais à six heures du soir. Trente minutes dans le car. Le trajet ne (12) m'a pas plu, parce que (8) c'était (4) fatigant (5). D'ailleurs, (6) c'était cher.

A l'hôtel, je (4) devais travailler à la réception. Tout le (1) temps, mes collègues (7) me demandaient (4) de faire du thé! Je (4) devais aussi écrire des lettres, nettoyer les chambres

---

4 correct use of imperfect tense

5 impressive vocabulary

6 good use of adverb

7 good use of pronoun

8 long sentence extended by 'parce que'

9 correct use of future tense

et servir les boissons dans le bar. J'aimais (4) surtout (6) le travail dans le bar, parce que (8) beaucoup des clients buvaient trop et c'était marrant (5) de les voir. En plus, (6) ils me (7) donnaient (4) des pourboires! Un client (7) m'a donné (2) vingt livres et avec l'argent j'achèterai (9) des vêtements et des cadeaux.

A l'avenir, (1) je ne veux pas travailler dans un hôtel parce que le travail est trop dur. Je voudrais (10) travailler à l'étranger dans une banque, parce que (8) le travail est plus facile, le climat est meilleur et en plus je pense qu'il sera facile de voler (11) de l'argent. Comme ça je serai (9) millionnaire! (200 words)

10 correct use of conditional

11 use of imagination

12 giving an opinion and justifying it

Your turn

Why not write a piece of coursework about your work experience? But don't just copy this one! Make up your own ideas, using some of the techniques shown above.

Published by Letts Educational
The Chiswick Centre
414 Chiswick High Road
London W4 5TF
tel: 020 89963333
fax: 020 87428390
e-mail: mail@lettsed.co.uk
website: www.letts-education.com

Letts Educational Limited is a division of Granada Learning Limited, part of Granada Plc.

© Terry Murray 2005

Design and illustration © Letts Educational Ltd 2005

First published 2005

ISBN 1 84315 4722

The author asserts his moral right to be identified as the author of this work.

British Library Cataloguing in Publication Data

A catalogue record for this book is available from the British Library.

Cover design by Big Top

Commissioned by Cassandra Birmingham

Project management for Letts by Julia Swales

Edited by Naomi Laredo, Small Print

Design and project management by Ken Vail Graphic Design, Cambridge

Printed and bound in Italy.